OSPREY AIRCRAFT OF THE ACES • 39

SPAD VII Aces of World War 1

SERIES EDITOR: TONY HOLMES

OSPREY AIRCRAFT OF THE ACES • 39

SPAD VII Aces of World War 1

Jon Guttman

OSPREY
AVIATION

Front cover
On 6 July 1917, Lts Armand de Turenne (in the SPAD VII in the foreground) and Georges Matton, commander of SPA48, were patrolling near Reims when they encountered six Albatros D Vs just over the French side of the frontline. Turenne eagerly attacked, but two of the German pilots quickly succeeded in getting on his tail. Coming to his aid, Matton managed to shoot one of the Albatros fighters down, and as the others fled back home, Turenne hit the engine of a second D V with an accurate burst of fire. His victim was Vfw Manfred Stimmel of *Jasta* 32, who force-landed between Courcy and Thil. Lt Matton attempted to land alongside the near-intact Albatros in an effort to prevent the pilot from sabotaging his machine, but the Frenchman's SPAD nosed over and he suffered minor injuries. Turenne later recalled;

'I circled over him (Stimmel) because I could see his propeller still turning. Then I saw the pilot jump out of the machine and lie on the ground while the aeroplane rolled along and crashed into a fence some 50 yards ahead. The German had sabotaged his machine according to orders.'

Vfw Stimmel was quickly taken prisoner, and the two downed German fighters were jointly credited to both SPAD pilots. These D Vs were Matton's eighth and ninth victories, and Turenne's third and fourth of an eventual tally of fifteen (*cover artwork by Iain Wyllie*)

Back cover
An unidentified pilot from N67 waits for the repair crew on the wing of his SPAD VII after a rough landing. This is apparently not eight-victory ace Maréchal-des-Logis Georges Flachaire's machine, although it has the same markings as his fighter – namely eyes on the cylinder fairings and a red fuselage band. Also of note are the square and circular cut-outs in the cowl panel, which were made in an effort to deal with the cooling problems that plagued early SPAD VIIs (*SHAA B81.2821 via Jon Guttman*)

First published in Great Britain in 2001, by Osprey Publishing, Elms Court, Chapel Way, Botley, Oxford, OX2 9LP
E-mail: info@ospreypublishing.com

ISBN 1 84176 222 9

Edited by Tony Holmes
Page design by TT Designs, T & B Truscott
Cover Artwork by Iain Wyllie
Aircraft Profiles by Harry Dempsey
Scale Drawings by Mark Styling
Origination by Grasmere Digital Imaging, Leeds, UK
Printed through Bookbuilders, Hong Kong

01 02 03 04 05   10 9 8 7 6 5 4 3 2 1

ACKNOWLEDGEMENTS
Thanks to the following airmen – all now 'Gone West' – whose recollections helped add a human touch to this tale of war; Arthur Raymond Brooks, Pierre Cardon, Pierre de Cazenove de Pradines, André Martenot de Cordoux and Louis Risacher. Thanks also to those colleagues whose invaluable assistance in the 'scavenger hunt' for photographs made this illustrated tome possible; Frank W Bailey, Norman L R Franks, Roberto Gentilli, Walter Pieters, Leslie A Rogers, Alan Toelle, Johan Visser, Aaron Weaver and Greg VanWyngarden.

EDITOR'S NOTE
To make this best-selling series as authoritative as possible, the Editor would be interested in hearing from any individual who may have relevant photographs, documentation or first-hand experiences relating to the elite fighter pilots, and their aircraft, of the various theatres of war. Any material used will be credited to its original source. Please write to Tony Holmes at 10 Prospect Road, Sevenoaks, Kent, TN13 3UA, Great Britain, or by e-mail at:
tony.holmes@osprey-jets.freeserve.co.uk

CONTENTS

INTRODUCTION

When World War 1 broke out in July 1914, military aviation was in its infancy and the concept of air superiority barely existed. By 1915, however, serious efforts were being made by airmen and aircraft designers of all the warring powers to devise a fighter capable of driving the other's aircraft from the skies above the frontlines. And by the middle of 1916, the essential fighter configuration had been established – a single-seater with a forward-firing machine gun, usually synchronised to fire through the propeller.

For the rest of the war aircraft manufacturers engaged in a constant struggle to improve the breed, seeking to gain a decisive edge in speed, rate of climb or manoeuvrability. Neither the Allies nor the Central Powers were able to attain that goal for long before the enemy would devise a new type that could equal or surpass the performance of the current world-beater. Among the few fighters that was able to hold its own in such a competitive environment was the French SPAD VII, which managed to remain in frontline service for more than two years.

An aeroplane's worth depends to a great degree upon its powerplant, and the water-cooled eight-cylinder marvel that Swiss engineer Marc Birkigt created in 1915 – the 150-hp Hispano-Suiza 8Aa – was to inspire several great Allied fighters, including the Royal Aircraft Factory SE 5 and SE 5a, and the Sopwith 5F.1 Dolphin. The first airframe to be mated to the 'Hisso', however, was that of the SPAD VII.

The French fighter had its origins in the dissolution of the *Societé provisoire des aéroplanes Deperdussin* and its resurrection in August 1914 as the *Societé anonyme pour l'Aviation et ses dérivés*, still retaining the original company acronym. In its new incarnation, SPAD also retained the services of Deperdussin's talented designer, Louis Béchereau.

Among Béchereau's first wartime designs was the SPAD SA.1, which sought to solve the problem of firing a machine gun past the propeller arc by placing a gunner in a pulpit held by means of struts in front of the propeller, and the aircraft's 80-hp Le Rhône 9C rotary engine.

Introduced in late 1915, the SA.1 and its successors – the SA.2 with a 110-hp Le Rhône 9J engine and the SA.4 which reverted to the 80-hp Le Rhône 9C due to cooling problems, and which featured ailerons on the upper wing only – were more terrifying to their gunners, who stood little chance of survival in the event of a nose-over upon landing, than to the enemy. The last of the SA types were removed from French service in May 1916, although as many as 67 continued to see action in Russia until as late as June 1917.

Although lacking a machine gun in its front pulpit, this SPAD SA.1 displays the basic airframe that would later be successfully mated to the 140-hp Hispano-Suiza 8Aa engine to create the SPAD VII.C1

SPAD's two-seat fighter was a failure, although the removal of the gunner's pulpit revealed a sound basic airframe. On 4 June 1915 Béchereau applied for a patent for the aeroplane's single-bay wing cellule, which featured intermediate struts of narrow chord, to which the bracing wires were attached at the midpoint. This arrangement added strength and, by reducing vibration in the wires, reduced drag as well.

Béchereau's next fighter, the SPAD SG, was essentially a single-seat SA.4 that replaced the gunner's pulpit with a remotely-controlled Hotchkiss gun in a nacelle mounted in front of the propeller. Evaluated in April 1916, it too was a failure, but then Béchereau altered the airframe to use the newly-developed 140 hp Hispano-Suiza 8A engine, and armed the fighter with a synchronised 0.303-in Vickers machine gun.

Originally designated the SPAD SH, the prototype had a large conical spinner in front of a circular radiator, and underwent flight testing in March 1916. The spinner was soon abandoned, but the rounded radiator shell was retained. A further development, using a 150-hp Hispano-Suiza 8Aa engine that was designated the SPAD V, underwent flight evaluation in July, reportedly reaching a maximum speed of 170 kph and climbing to 3000 metres in nine minutes. Already impressed with its fundamental design, the *Aviation Militaire* placed an order for 268 aircraft on 10 May 1916. The final production variant was officially designated the SPAD VII.C1 (the 'C1' indicating that it was a single-seat *chasseur*, or fighter), although it was more widely known as the SPAD VII.

Allegedly the first frontline pilot to be issued with a SPAD VII was Lt Armand Pinsard, commander of N26, who is believed to have been allocated S122 as early as 23 August. Pinsard's principal claim to fame up until then had been his escape from a German prison camp. Forced down behind enemy lines on 8 February 1915, he had spent almost 14 months as a PoW when he escaped with Capitaine Victor Menard on 26 March 1916 and crossed the frontline to safety on 10 April.

On 1 November 1916 Pinsard downed an enemy aeroplane over Lechelle for his first victory. Later that month he left N26 to take command of N78, with whom he would claim a further 15 German aircraft destroyed before being injured in a flying accident on 12 June 1917. Upon recovery, Pinsard took command of SPA23 early in 1918, increasing his score to 27 by 22 August. Eight days later he was made an *Officier de la Légion d'Honneur*, and by the end of the war he had also been awarded the *Croix de Guerre* with 19 *Palmes* and the British Military

Lt Armand Pinsard of *Escadrille* N26 was among the first frontline pilots to fly the SPAD VII, allegedly experiencing his first combat in S122 on 26 August 1916. His first confirmed victory with the fighter was not scored until 1 November, however

These SPAD VIIs were all assigned to SPA78, which Capitaine Pinsard led from November 1916 through to 12 June 1917, when he was injured in an accident. The dark-coloured fighter furthest from the camera was almost certainly Pinsard's SPAD, which had an all-black fuselage adorned with the legend *Revanche* in white. The remaining SPADs all bear SPA78's black panther insignia, along with individual numerals on the fuselage and upper wing (*via Greg VanWyngarden*)

SPA112's aircraft had two red fuselage bands and personal motifs of the pilot's choice – such as the white and red tail décor on this SPAD VII of Sous-Lt Victor Régnier. The future ace scored his first victory in concert with N124's Adjudant Norman Prince on 9 September 1916, although soon after downing a balloon for his fifth kill on 6 April 1917, Régnier was severely wounded and evacuated to the rear

Cross. Pinsard continued to serve with distinction during World War 2, leading *Groupe de Combat* (GC) 21 until he was wounded in a bombing raid on 6 June 1940, resulting in the loss of a leg (see *Osprey Aircraft of the Aces 28 - French Aces of World War 2* for further details). Pinsard died at Ceyzeriat on 10 May 1953 during a dinner being held by *Les Vielles Tiges* association.

Another early SPAD VII recipient, Sgt Paul Sauvage of *Escadrille* N65, had already scored three victories when he received S112 on 2 September 1916. He claimed his fourth on 23 September and his fifth on 2 October, followed by a sixth on 2 November. A Rumpler fell to his guns on 10 December, and on the 27th he downed an Albatros over Moronvillers. Outstanding though Sauvage's performance was, it was somewhat over-shadowed in N65 by his more flamboyant squadronmate, Sous-Lt Charles Nungesser (see *Osprey Aircraft of the Aces 33 - Nieuport Aces of World War 1* for further details), who preferred to keep flying the slower, less sturdy but more manoeuvrable Nieuport 17, and whose score at that time stood at 21. Sauvage, known to the French as *'le benjamin des As'* because of his youth, would add no more to his tally before being killed by an exploding anti-aircraft shell 20 miles east of Maissonette on 7 January 1917 – one month short of his 20th birthday.

Yet another French airman whose exploits earned him the privilege of flying one of the earliest SPAD VIIs was Adjudant Maxime Lenoir, who had scored his first victory over an Aviatik two-seater while flying a Caudron G IV with *Escadrille* C18 on 5 June 1915, followed by a balloon ten days later. After retraining on Nieuports, he was reassigned to N23, and claimed nine more victories between 17 March and 25 September 1916, when he was wounded in the process of downing an enemy three-seater. Upon receiving SPAD VII S116, Lenoir decorated it with the letters *LE* over a black man's head, forming a rebus of his own name under the cockpit, and the legend TROMPE LA MORT ('death cheater') on the fuselage. Alas, Lenoir's death-defying decor proved to be premature, for he was shot down and killed on 25 October 1916.

THE STORKS

One of the earliest SPAD VIIs to reach operational units was S115, which was in turn assigned to Sous-Lt Georges Guynemer of N3 *'les Cigognes'* ('the Storks') on 2 September 1916. The 21-year-old Guynemer was already N3's leading ace, and he wasted no time in putting S115 through its paces – on 4 September he downed an Aviatik C II over Hyencourt for his 15th victory, his victims being Ltns Hans Steiner and Otto Fresenius of *Kampfstaffel* 37.

Twenty-four SPAD VIIs reached the front during the course of September, and N3's aces (who had already mastered the manoeuvrable but tricky Nieuports) quickly amended their tactics to take advantage of the new fighter's speed.

On 23 September Guynemer downed two Fokkers – plus a third that went unconfirmed – within five minutes of each other, but as he returned over the lines at an altitude of 3000 metres, his new aeroplane was struck by a 75 mm shell fired by nervous French anti-aircraft gunners. With the SPAD VII's water reservoir shattered and fabric torn away from its left upper wing, the fighter spun down, but Guynemer managed to regain control and pull up at about 180 metres above the ground, before crash-landing in a shell hole and emerging with a cut knee and a slight concussion. In spite of his painful injuries, he stood at attention when the troops who had come to rescue him recognised *'Le Grand Georges'* and immediately organised a salute for him, complete with a round of *La Marseillaise*.

Sgt Georges Guynemer prepares for take-off in his first SPAD VII (S115) in September 1916 (*via Greg VanWyngarden*)

This rare in-flight photograph shows Guynemer at the controls of S115. In addition to N3's stork emblem and the ace's number 2 on the fuselage (both in red), the fighter also featured blue, white and red fuselage bands and the legend *"Vieux Charles"* below the cockpit (*via Greg VanWyngarden*)

When later describing the incident to his father, Guynemer gave his appraisal of the aeroplane that he credited with his seemingly miraculous survival;

'Only the fuselage was left, but it was intact. The SPAD is solid – with another (aeroplane), I would now be thinner than this piece of paper.'

He was completely sold on the new fighter, and soon returned to action after receiving S132 on 25 September.

April 1917 saw the last Nieuports withdrawn from N3, which was

redesignated SPA3. Scores of other French *escadrilles* would soon follow suit, but SPA3 would remain the most famous of them all. With 175 confirmed victories by the end of the war, it was the highest-scoring unit in the *Aviation Française*. As the unit's leading light, Guynemer was the second-ranking French ace, and because of his selfless devotion to his country, he was more lionised by his countrymen than the self-serving pilot who would eventually surpass him, René Fonck. Close behind Guynemer in French hearts were several other high-ranking aces of SPA3, namely Dorme, Heurtaux, Deullin, Tenant de la Tour and Auger.

Born in Paris on 5 December 1883, Mathieu Marie Joseph Antoine Tenant de la Tour had been a cavalry officer before transferring to aviation. He first served in N57, flaming a balloon on 25 January 1916 and being made a *Chevalier de la Légion d'Honneur* on 1 February. He was wounded in action on 25 April, and upon his recovery he was reassigned to N3, where (flying Nieuports) he had raised his score to seven by 6 September. De la Tour probably scored his eighth victory – a Halberstadt – over Brié-St Christ while flying a SPAD VII on 27 December 1916, his victim on that occasion being Leutnant der Reserve Gustav Leffers of *Jasta* 1, a nine-victory recipient of the *Ordure Pour le Mérite*.

In April 1917 de la Tour was promoted to lieutenant and given command of N26, with whom he downed an enemy aeroplane on 7 May. This victory was the ace's ninth, and last, for he was killed in an accident at Auchel while flying a new SPAD XIII on 17 December 1917.

Born in Baucourt-les-Souppleville, Meuse, on 30 January 1894, Maréchal-des-Logis René Pierre Marie Dorme was serving in the *7e Groupe d'Artillerie à Pied* at Bizerte, in Tunisia, when World War 1 began, and he promptly requested a transfer into aviation. After training, Dorme was assigned to *Escadrille* C94 on 5 June 1915, flying Caudron G IVs. His first brush with the enemy in the air occurred on 13 March 1916, and he was cited for probably downing a German aeroplane. Dorme's demonstrated aggressiveness also earned him a transfer to N3.

The future ace expressed his desire to liberate the territory occupied by the Germans after the Franco-Prussian War of 1871 by marking his SPAD with the cross of Lorraine. Dorme's hatred for the enemy never got the better of his judgement, however, and the relative maturity of his behaviour in combat gained him the nickname of 'Père' Dorme, which he also obligingly marked below the cockpit of his fighter.

After teaming up with Lt Alfred Heurtaux to shoot down an LVG on 9 July (credited as the first confirmed victory for both pilots), Dorme was awarded the *Médaille Militaire*, and on 18 October he was made a *Chevalier de la Légion d'Honneur*.

René Fonck of neighbouring *Escadrille* N103 recalled that the 'Storks' were strict about confirmations and that if a pilot's claim was not confirmed, 'he owed a big fine to the officers' mess, where his

Sous-Lt René Dorme (right) poses alongside his SPAD VII S314 *PERE DORME IV* – note the the green Cross of Lorraine on the fighter's upper decking. Not visible in this view is his small number 12 aft of the red and white stork emblem. Dorme scored 23 official victories – and numerous others that went unconfirmed – prior to being killed in action on 25 May 1917 by Ltn Heinrich Kroll of *Jasta* 9. Dorme was the German's fifth victim, thus giving him ace status

Lt Alfred Heurtaux of SPA3 stands before an early SPAD VII. One of the types' earliest exponents, Heurtaux brought down a total of 21 opponents, including German ace Ltn Kurt Wintgens

boasting covered him with ridicule'. That all seemed a moot point to Dorme, who according to Fonck, and others who knew him, would typically mention a success only when directly questioned. 'Well, yes – over there! I left one in flames at that place'. *Escadrille* records indicated that Dorme engaged in 120 combats and officially downed 23 German aircraft. His squadron-mates believed that at least 20 of his 50 'probables' would have been awarded to him as definite kills had he cared enough to co-operate in getting them confirmed.

Dorme was credited with four victories in September 1916, and had undoubtedly painted his number 12 and cross of Lorraine on his own SPAD VII by October, when he added three more to his score. He downed a Rumpler on 16 November and a Fokker on 4 December, and opened his account for 1917 with an AEG north-east of Fismes on 31 March. Three more Germans fell victim to '*Père*' Dorme in April, as did a three-seater on 4 May and an Albatros two-seater on 10 May. At that point, only one ace in SPA3 had a tally that exceeded Dorme's total of 23 victories – Guynemer, with 38.

Alfred Heurtaux was born in Nantes on 20 May 1893. He underwent the classic training of a professional officer, starting with admission in 1912 to the Military School at Saint Cyr – the French equivalent of Sandhurst or West Point – followed that October by an obligatory year of service as a *soldat* in the *4e Régiment d'Hussards*. Heurtaux entered St Cyr as an aspirant in October 1913, but when war broke out he joined the *9e Hussards* and got his commission on 4 August 1914.

Sous-Lt Heurtaux soon lived up to the trust implicit in his rapid promotion, being cited three times in four months for valour on the battlefield. Nevertheless, he decided that the Western Front was no place for light cavalry, and on 6 December 1914 his application was accepted to train on the new alternative – aircraft.

After serving in MS26 as an observer, he trained as a pilot and received his brevet on 29 May 1915. Assigned to MS38, Heurtaux was promoted to lieutenant on 25 December 1915, and on 5 June 1916 he obtained a transfer to N3, assuming command of the unit on 16 June.

As previously mentioned, Heurtaux began his scoring with an LVG shared with Dorme on 9 July, and by 17 August he had become an ace – as well as being made a *Chevalier de la Légion d'Honneur* on 4 August.

There can be little doubt that Heurtaux had switched from Nieuports to the SPAD VII by 15 September, when he scored his sixth victory over St Pierre-Vaast. A Roland C II fell to his gun two days later, and on 25 September he destroyed a 'Fokker' over Villers Carbonnel. The latter turned out to be a Halberstadt D II flown by Ltn Kurt Wintgens of *Jasta* 1, an 18-victory ace, and holder of the *Ordure Pour le Mérite*.

Heurtaux's score rose steadily thereafter – two victories in October, three in November and another three in late December. He claimed a 'double' on 24 January 1917, and downed another enemy aeroplane the next day. Yet another German aircraft fell near Bois de Faulx on 6 February, and an Albatros two-seater was claimed over Beaurieux on 4 May, bringing Heurtaux's official total to 21, as well as 13 'probables'.

Albert Louis Deullin was born in Epernay on 24 August 1890, and entered the military at an early age. Serving in the *31e Régiment de Dragons* when war broke out, he later transferred to the *8e Dragons* and was commissioned a sous-lieutenant in December 1914. Switching to aviation in April 1915, he received Pilot's Brevet No 2078 on 14 June and was assigned to MF62 on 2 July.

Deullin (with observer, Capitaine Alphonse Colcomb) scored his first kill during a reconnaissance deep into enemy territory on 10 February 1916, and he was transferred to N3 soon after. By the end of March 1916 he had destroyed two more enemy aircraft, although he was wounded in combat on 2 April. Returning to action 15 days later, Deullin scored his fourth victory on the 30th and was made a *Chevalier de la Légion d'Honneur* on 4 June.

He claimed his seventh kill on 15 September, by which time SPADs were entering the *escadrille* inventory, and still more enemy aircraft fell to him on 22 September, and on 10 and 23 November. After scoring his 11th success over a two-seater on 10 February 1917, Deullin left N3 to take command of N73 12 days later, and by 8 November he had raised his tally to 19. On 7 February 1918 Capitaine Deullin was promoted to command GC19, although he continued to actively lead, downing an Albatros east of Montdidier on 19 May for his 20th, and final, victory.

In addition to being elevated to an *Officier de la Légion d'Honneur* for his leadership on 23 June 1918, Deullin was awarded the *Croix de Guerre* with 14 *Palmes*. Although he survived the war, he did not enjoy the hard-earned fruits of victory for long – on 29 May 1929, Deullin was killed while test-flying an aircraft prototype at Villacoublay aerodrome.

Another famous 'stork', Alfred Victor Robert Auger was born in Constantine on 26 January 1889 and was serving as a sous-lieutenant in the *31ème Régiment d'Infanterie* when war broke out. Wounded in action on 31 August 1914, he was soon made a *Chevalier de la Légion d'Honneur*.

After further duty in the infantry, Auger opted for the air service and began flight training at Pau in February 1915, earning Military Pilot's Brevet No 614. Assigned to C11, he was wounded on 8 July, and in August requested fighter training in Nieuports. On 22 September he was made CO of N31 and promoted to capitaine in December. Auger scored his first kill (an LVG two-seater) on 13 March 1916, followed by an Albatros on 2 April, but he was severely injured in an accident on 16 April.

After recovering, Auger was transferred to N3 and issued one of the *escadrille's* remaining Nieuports, which he used to shoot down an

Yet another famous Stork of N3, Lt Albert Deullin stands before a SPAD VII in company with the *escadrille*'s mascot, 'Parasol'. Having raised his score to ten kills by 23 November 1916, Deullin was then given command of SPA73 on 23 February 1917, and of GC19 on 7 February 1918

Albatros near Rogerville on 9 February 1917, killing the pilot, Offizier-stellvertreter Richard Krone of *Kampfgeschwader* 2. Having thus proven his mettle, Capitaine Auger relieved Heurtaux as the *escadrille* commander on 17 March, and presumably was given a SPAD VII as well.

On the previous day, President of the Republic Raymond Poincaré had arrived at N3's aerodrome at Manoncourt to present Guynemer with the Russian Order of St George, 4th Class. Prior to the president's arrival, however, Guynemer had set out on a solo patrol, and by the time he returned he had downed a Roland D II of *Jasta* 32b (whose wounded pilot, Ltn Rudi Lothar Freiherr von Hausen, was taken prisoner) and two Albatros two-seaters – the first triple victory by a French pilot.

Auger resumed his scoring on 22 April with a two-seater over Lierval, and on 11 May he and Lt Xavier de Sevin of N12 shot down another two-seater over Vailly. The destruction of two more enemy aircraft on 4 and 28 June brought Auger's score up to seven.

Such, then, were the airmen who first blooded the SPAD VII in N3, adding considerably to laurels already won in the Nieuport, and establishing the unit as the top-scoring squadron in the *Aviation Française*. By the end of 1916, however, N3 was not the only unit whose aircraft bore the by-then famous 'stork' insignia on their fuselage side. On 1 November, N3 became the nucleus of a *groupe de combat* (which included N26, N73 and N103) that was formed to achieve local air superiority. Designated GC12, it would be led by former N3 commander Capitaine Antonin Brocard.

With the formation of the new *Groupe des Cigognes*, the other squadrons' previous unit insignia (such as N26's flaming torch and N103's red star) were replaced by storks in different attitudes of flight. Some variation was also employed in additional markings, such as

Adjutant André Chainat is seen in the cockpit of his SPAD VII, *"l'Oiseau Bleu 6"*, shortly before being badly wounded in action on 7 September 1916. Never to see action again, Chainet scored 11 victories in total (*Service Historique de l'Armée de l'Air B76.1365 via Jon Guttman*)

Adjutant Benjamin Bozon-Verduraz (left) and Cpl Louis Risacher pose beside a SPAD VII at Bergues-sur-Mer in the late summer of 1917. The aircraft's cowling panels have been removed and circular holes drilled in the radiator cowl to improve cooling

diagonal fuselage bands, which were blue, white and red for SPA3, red and white for SPA26 and SPA103, and blue and white (the colours of the Virgin Mary) for SPA73.

SPA103 retained the red Roman numerals by which its individual aircraft were identified, and many of its aircraft had its old unit emblem – the red star – applied to the upper right wing. Finally, during the summer of 1917, SPA3 often used green, rather than the more usual red, for the Arabic numbers that identified its individual aircraft.

Few units associated their pilots with numerals to the degree that SPA3 did. By the end of 1916, '1' was associated with Brocard, '2' adorned nearly all of Guynemer's aircraft, '3' was Deullin's number, '6' was Sgt André Chainat's, '7' was Auger's, '8' was Adjutant Joseph-Henri Guiguet's, '9' was Capitaine Georges Raymond's, '11' was Heurtaux's and '12' was Dorme's.

Personal touches included Guynemer's famous legend *"VIEUX CHARLES"* beneath his cockpit, as well as Chainat's *"l'OISEAU BLEU 6"*, Guiguet's *'P'tit Jo'* and Raymond's *"MA NINON"*. In addition to the legend *PERE DORME IV*, Dorme's aeroplane had a green Cross of Lorraine painted on the fuselage upper decking, while Auger's SPAD VII had the name *"Je"* and a German being speared on the beak of his stork.

Guynemer also applied some creative flair to the sound of his engine. Whenever he returned to the aerodrome after downing an enemy, he would open and close the throttle of his Hispano-Suiza engine to produce a humming sound that resembled the words *'J'en ai en'* ('I got one of them').

Cpl Louis Risacher, a Parisian-born infantryman-turned flight instructor who managed to wangle a posting to SPA3 on 23 June 1917, described life in GC12;

'Living conditions were very rough. Brocard used to put us in barracks without comfort, sometimes in tents when other groups were living in châteaux or houses. We were sent wherever there was a French offensive, or where a German attack was expected. Brocard thought too much comfort would be bad for us, and wanted to keep us tough. We had a cook who used to go to town and get food. We ate beefsteak, potatoes, vegetables, wine and water. We had a bar, but used it very little.'

Although Risacher was a superb aviator, he did not come into his stride as a fighter pilot until 16 May 1918, when he and his best friend in SPA3, Sous-Lt Benjamin Bozon-Verduraz, shared in downing an enemy aeroplane over Montdidier. By then, SPA3 was equipped with the SPAD XIII, in which Risacher would ultimately bring his score up to five and Bozon-Verduraz would finish the war with eleven victories.

While SPA3's heroes dominated the French aviation press, the other 'Stork' squadrons of GC12 produced their own share of aces too.

Maréchal-des-Logis Constant Fréderic Soulier stands beside a SPAD VII of SPA26. Born in Paris on 5 September 1897, Soulier joined N26 on 15 June 1916, and was still three months short of his 20th birthday when he scored his sixth victory on 3 June 1917 (*SHAA B87.197 via Jon Guttman*)

N69's Lieutenant Honoré Marie Joseph Léon Guillaume de Bonald sits in the cockpit of his SPAD VII. The ace's four-leaf clover marking can be clearly seen on the fuselage, although the legend *'Willy'* (apparently his nickname) is obscured by the upper wing shadow. The latter marking appeared on the fuselage under the left side of the cockpit on all his aircraft. De Bonald scored four victories in France before being wounded on 14 June 1917, and sometime after rejoining N69 on 3 November 1917, he scored a fifth kill over Italy. In addition to being made a *Chevalier de la Légion d'Honneur* on 15 June 1917, he received the *Croix de Guerre* with five *Palmes* and the *Italian Medaglia d'Argento por Valore Militare*

Maréchal-des-Logis Constant Roger Fréderic Soulier had claimed three victories with N26 in 1916 before being hospitalised on 14 January 1917. After returning to N26 on 12 March 1917, the 19-year-old Soulier resumed scoring on 14 May, and on the 27th of that month he downed a DFW C V to become the youngest ace since the late Paul Sauvage. His sixth confirmed victory – out of 15 claimed – was another DFW, shared with Lieutenant Honoré de Bonald of N69 and Sgt Chapelle of N31 on 3 June. On 29 June, however, Soulier was hospitalised once again, and he never returned to combat.

Another ace of *Escadrille* 26 was Adjutant Gustave Naudin, who scored his first victory in a Caudron in concert with his observer-gunner,

Sous-Lt Jean Marie, while serving in C224 on 12 July 1917. Subsequently transferred to SPA26, Naudin downed a second enemy aeroplane on 29 December, but was probably flying SPAD XIIIs when he achieved his last four successes in 1918. Serving in the infantry during World War 2 (and wounded in action on 9 September 1944), Naudin rose to the rank of capitaine and was made an *Officier de la Légion d'Honneur* in 1945. He died on 16 April 1978 at the age 87.

N73 acquired its first SPAD VIIs in January 1917. Aside from Capitaine Deullin, who took command on 22 February, the only aces to score while serving in SPA73 were American Charles J Biddle of the *Lafayette* Flying Corps and François Battesti.

Born in Azzana, Corsica, on 4 May 1890, François Marie Noël Battesti served in the infantry before entering aviation on 1 January 1914, receiving Military Pilot's Brevet No 453 on 3 April, and flying Blériot XIs in *escadrilles* BL18 and BL3 pre-war. After wartime service in Caudron G IVs with C10, Sous-Lt Battesti was reassigned to N73 on 12 March 1917, and claimed his first kill on 24 April. He was probably flying SPAD VIIs when he was credited with his second victory on 4 July and his third on 12 November. In 1918, he added a further three kills to his tally while flying SPAD XIIIs and a solitary victory with the 37 mm cannon-armed SPAD XII.

Like many of the aces he knew and admired in SPA3, Battesti used the same personal number – '11' – on all the fighters he flew. Made a *Chevalier de la Légion d'Honneur*, he published a small memoir, *Les cigognes de Brocard en combat*, two years before passing away in his home town of Azzana on 24 August 1977.

American *Lafayette* Flying Corps volunteer Cpl Charles J Biddle poses beside his SPAD VII, marked with a red 8, the *cigogne au style japonais* and the blue and white band of SPA73. Taught the deadly art of aerial combat by his commander, Capitaine Deullin, Biddle was flying a SPAD XIII when he scored his first victory – an Albatros two-seater – on 5 December 1917. Transferring to the US Army Air Service several months later, he flew SPAD VIIs once again with the 103rd Aero Squadron, then led the 13th Aero Squadron before ending the war as CO of the 4th Pursuit Group, Biddle's final tally was eight victories

Sous-Lt René Fonck peers into the cockpit of his SPAD VII (S1461) after a rough landing in May 1917. Of note are the extra perforations forward of the standard cowling louvres to aid in cooling the engine. Just visible on the upper wing is the old red star of N103, whilst the fuselage side reveals Fonck's red number IX superimposed on an earlier number XV

Two aces flew SPAD VIIs in SPA103. Sgt Claude Haegelen probably downed an enemy aeroplane on 3 May 1917, and scored confirmed victories on 27 and 28 May, but was wounded on the latter date. After recuperating, he was assigned to SPA100 on 11 March 1918, and went on to claim the bulk of his 22 victories with this unit. When Adjutant-Chef René Paul Fonck joined SPA103, however, he came to stay.

Born in Saulcy-le-Meurthe on 27 March 1894, Fonck trained at Lyon to receive Military Pilot's Brevet No 1979 on 15 May 1915. Assigned to C47, Fonck demonstrated early on that he would not be content merely to fly reconnaissance missions when he mounted a Lewis machine gun to fire over the upper wing of his Caudron G IV. On 3 August 1916, he and his observer, Lt Thiberge, attacked and shot down a Rumpler two-seater, and on 17 March 1917, Fonck and Lt Marcaggi downed an Albatros. His demonstrated aggressiveness convinced his superiors to transfer him to a fighter unit, and on 25 April he arrived at GC12's aerodrome at Bonne Maison. Fonck later wrote in his autobiography, *Mes Combats*;

'I had obtained a new aeroplane, naturally – a brand-new SPAD with which I promised myself to do a great job. It took me two days to put it into shape with my mechanics, Delmas and Poirrier.'

After a false start or two, Fonck's careful preparations paid off over Laon on 5 May;

'There were nine aeroplanes in the action – five Boches and four French – deployed in a narrow space. Quickly we rose from the mist that formed a thick fog and enveloped us. In the midst of it we risked, at any moment, meeting each other in a deadly collision.

'Sgt (Pierre) Schmitter was the first one hit. His aeroplane, riddled in several places, also took a bullet in the motor.

'Sgt Haegelen and Lt Hervet succeeded momentarily in relieving him, but in their turn they were getting the worst of it when I arrived to change the course of events. Twice I attacked the Boches who were machine-gunning my friends. Despite the skilful manoeuvring that they exhibited, I succeeded in firing at one of the Boches at point-blank range. He had come out of a cloud in front of me. To tell the truth the opportunity came from heaven. With a well-directed burst I put an end to his career.

'His aeroplane immediately nose-dived and crashed in the corner of a wooded area. I followed him in his descent while the other two French "Storks" were pursuing the Fokkers, whose flight was suddenly accelerated as they turned tail and made for home. This victory of mine was not contested. So many witnesses had been present that it was immediately confirmed.'

Fonck's emphasis on witnesses referred to a victory he had claimed two days earlier, which remained unconfirmed due to the lack of corroborating evidence. If his writing hints at vanity, so did his demeanour around his fellow pilots. He did not mix well with others, behaving either withdrawn and shy, or conceited – both traits indicative of a deep-seated sense of insecurity.

Fonck's self-aggrandising tendencies annoyed many of his fellow pilots, and undermined their respect for him in spite of his very real achievements. In seeming contradiction to his unsympathetic personality, however, Fonck's lifestyle was arguably among the most mature for a fighter pilot of his time. While Guynemer flew relentlessly, and third-ranking French ace Charles Nungesser alternated between fighting, womanising and drinking, with barely two hours of sleep at night, Fonck rested between missions, drank moderately and spent much of his leisure time practising his marksmanship.

Fonck downed an Albatros on 11 May and 'made ace' two days later. Over the next two months he only added one more Albatros to his score (on 12 June), but subsequently destroyed one enemy aeroplane a day between 19 and 22 August. At that point, Fonck's deeds could well have spoken for him – if only he had let them.

Louis Risacher recalled an incident, during a visit from Royal Flying Corps pilots in the summer of 1917 to familiarise GC12's personnel with British aircraft, which vividly displayed the particular talents and fighting styles of Guynemer and Fonck;

'There was a Canadian I remember, one of their aces – I cannot remember his name. He offered to have a mock dogfight with Fonck and Guynemer. Guynemer had the first "fight". It was decided by Guynemer and the Canadian ace that they would cross in the air and the "combat" would begin at once. Immediately, Guynemer was on his tail and he could not get him off. He was a fine chap, the Canadian. He came to Guynemer and said, *'J'ai été tué beaucoups des fois!'* ('That was sport!'). He was flying a Camel. Guynemer had outmanoeuvred a Camel in a SPAD – absolutely!

'Fonck said, "Send me three pilots, and I will attack them. They will never see me". Three English pilots started, and were over the field, where we lost sight of Fonck. Suddenly, there was a SPAD flying through the three Englishmen. It was Fonck. That was the difference between the two schools. Fonck was a very good pilot, of course, but he never made a dogfighting manoeuvre in the air – he always flew flat. Not to be seen by anybody – that was his style.'

If the early months of 1917 saw the Storks at the peak of their glory, the period between May and September 1917 would see several of their leading lights extinguished one by one.

Intensive aerial activity in May began with Guynemer downing an Albatros over Courtecon on the 2nd. The next day, Heurtaux shot the wings off an Albatros two-seater over Fismes for his 21st victory, while Guynemer and Dorme each added one to their tallies on 4 May. Guiguet scored his fourth victory over Mont Châlons on 5 May, but during a fight with nine Albatros D IIIs that same day, Heurtaux lived up to his nickname 'The Bullet Catcher' when he was shot through both thighs, his skull was creased by a bullet and another round passed through both cheeks. Semi-conscious from loss of blood, he just managed to crash-land in Allied lines and was rushed to a field hospital.

Heurtaux's friend, Dorme, avenged him by downing a two-seater on the 10th, and Auger 'made ace' on the 11th, but on the 23rd Guiguet returned to the aerodrome badly wounded by a shell fragment.

Guiguet, commissioned as a sous-lieutenant, finally returned to action on 29 August 1918 with newly-formed addition to GC12, *Escadrille* SPA167. Whilst serving with this unit, he and his commander, Lt Bernard Barny de Romanet, destroyed a two-seater on 24 October to take Romanet's tally to 17 and give Guiguet his all-important fifth victory.

SPA3 suffered a profound shock on 25 May when the seemingly invincible 'Père' Dorme failed to return. He, Brocard and Deullin were on patrol when they encountered a flight of Albatros D IIIs of *Jasta* 9. In the fight that ensued, Deullin thought he saw Dorme shoot down an opponent in flames before he himself came under attack by four Albatros scouts. When he next saw Dorme, the latter was being driven further into German-held territory, but by then Deullin was too low on ammunition and fuel to do anything but fight his way back to base. Later that morning, a Bréguet reconnaissance aeroplane reported sighting a French fighter burning on the ground.

Dorme's fate was further described in a diary entry on 11 June 1917, in which Leutnant der Reserve Heinrich Claudius Kroll of *Jasta* 9 (see *Osprey Aircraft of the Aces 32 - Albatros Aces of World War 1* for further details) expressed his elation at learning the identity of a French opponent he had brought down;

'I shot him down near Fort la Pompelle near Reims. It was a very hot circling fight that started at 5300 metres and lasted down to 800 metres. He suddenly dived vertically and burst into flames when he hit the ground. Dorme's identity was confirmed by means of a watch with an inscription on the cover: "Presented by the Lip factory at Besançon to Monsieur René Dorme in remembrance of his heroic achievements during the war".'

Kroll, for whom Dorme had been his fifth victory, later went on to command Royal Saxon *Jasta* 24, increase his tally to 33 kills and be awarded the *Ordure Pour le Mérite*, before being put out of the war with a grievous shoulder wound on 14 August 1918.

While Dorme's loss was unsettling to the Storks, 25 May had also seen Guynemer become the first French pilot to bring down four enemy aeroplanes during the course of a day – to which he added another 24 hours later. Although still in pain from his wounds, fellow ace Heurtaux was back in the air by the end of June.

Then, on 12 July, GC12 was ordered to move from Bonne Maison to Bierne, near Bergues, in Flanders. The RFC could have told the French how dangerous a sector they were entering (some of the best German *Jagdstaffeln* were concentrated there), although they soon discovered this for themselves. On 28 July Auger attacked five enemy fighters over Wocsten-Zuideschoote and was duly shot in the neck. By sheer will, he managed to disengage and reach Allied lines, but died of his wound moments later. On 7 August, Heurtaux was made CO of SPA3.

August saw more scoring by the Storks, including kills by Guynemer in his new 37 mm cannon-armed SPAD XII, as well as a visit from King Albert of Belgium, who awarded the *Croix de Chevalier de l'Ordre de Léopold* to Guynemer and Heurtaux. On 20 August, Maj-Gen Hugh Trenchard presented the Distinguished Service Order to Guynemer on behalf of the RFC.

During a fight on 3 September, Heurtaux was shot through the femoral artery, and he would have bled to death in the air had the incendiary bullet that passed through his thigh not cauterised the wound, permitting him to reach Allied lines. Heurtaux's fighting career was at an end, however.

One week later, another hero from an adjacent *groupe* fought his last aerial duel. After scoring his first victory while in N57 on 29 July 1916, Capitaine Jean Georges Fernand Matton had been transferred to take

Still suffering from the grievous leg wound that ended his fighting career on 3 September 1917, Capitaine Heurtaux needed two canes for support when he attended an awards ceremony in 1918 (*via Greg VanWyngarden*)

command of N48, and whilst with this unit he brought his score up to nine, including two enemy fighters on 6 July 1917. GC11, then comprising SPA12, SPA31, SPA48 and SPA57, accompanied GC12 to Flanders later in July, but there Matton, too, became a casualty of the intense fighting over that sector, being killed on 10 September by Leutnant der Reserve Josef Jacobs, commander of *Jasta 7* (see *Osprey Aircraft of the Aces 40 - Fokker Dr I Aces of World War 1* for further details).

The most staggering loss to the French was yet to come. On 11 September, Georges Guynemer, then France's leading ace with 53 victories to his credit, was flying a new SPAD XIII with twin machine guns when he failed to return from a patrol with Bozon-Verduraz. The Germans later credited his demise to Lt Kurt Wissemann of *Jasta 3*, Guynemer being his fifth victim.

'The Storks' reaction to the news of Guynemer's death was that 'we would fly more and more to avenge him', declared Risacher. 'We would kill every German we could. Bozon-Verduraz and myself, despite the disappearance of Guynemer, wanted to see that the Storks had the same successes as when he was alive'. The cumulative loss of Guynemer, Heurtaux, Auger and Dorme must have had a psychological impact on SPA3, however, for the *escadrille* only scored two victories for the rest of 1917, including Raymond's fourth on 27 October.

At neighbouring SPA103, René Fonck also swore to avenge Guynemer, and on 14 September he downed a two-seater in flames over Langemarck. 'Such was the funeral of Guynemer to me', he later wrote. As he approached GC12's aerodrome, Fonck announced his 12th victory by manipulating the throttle to produce the *'J'en ai en'* sound that had been the late Guynemer's signature.

Whatever his intent, his fellow Storks viewed it resentfully as a tactless act, and some reproached him for it to his face. Fonck did not reply to his detractors. 'It is not part of my make-up to emulate the deeds of others', he wrote, and spent the next month-and-a-half perfecting his fighting skills, shooting down six more enemy aeroplanes by 27 October.

This line-up of SPAD VIIs from SPA3, seen at Bonne Maison aerodrome on 5 July 1917, includes (from the aircraft nearest to the camera) S413 '2', flown by Capitaine Guynemer, S1329, S1416 '6', flown by Capitaine Alfred Auger, S1339 '7', Guynemer's cannon-armed SPAD XII Ca.1 S382 (without wings), S1422 '9', flown by Lt Georges Raymond, S1639 '10', flown by Sous-Lt Henri Rabatel (four victories), S424 and S420 '13'

GC12 left Flanders for Maisonneuve on 11 November, and moved to Beauzée-sur-Aire, near Souilly in the *IVe Armée* sector, on 17 January 1918. When SPA3 resumed its scoring on 16 February, it was predominantly equipped with the SPAD XIII. Although the unit produced more aces in that year (the most prominent of whom was American Frank Baylies, with 12 victories), SPA3's glory days had passed. The 'Stork' who came most fully into his own in 1918 would be SPA103's deadly hunter, Fonck.

— BETTER COOLING AND A HOTTER ENGINE —

In spite of its early successes, the SPAD VII revealed some problems, the most irritating of which was the inefficiency of its radiator and cooling vents, which resulted in cold engines in the winter and overheating in the summer. Various field expedients were tried, such as drilling holes in the tight cowling or removing the cowling vents entirely.

Adjutant Pierre de Cazenove de Pradines of N81 described an example of mechanical trouble;

'The carburettor of my SPAD was badly adjusted. Having heated going up, it cooled down in level flight, coughed, then stalled. Having found a convenient field under my wings, I landed next to an anti-aircraft battery. The artillerymen welcomed me with delight, but I cut short their welcome and telephoned the aircraft park to come and repair my motor. By the time the repairs were effected it was too dark to take off. I had to spend the night there, and the next morning I succeeded in getting started.

'I tried to take off, but the heavy rain of the night before had rendered the field muddy and my rolling wheels kicked up soil, which broke my prop. A return visit was made to the air park, and once more I was stuck in this position. The third day it was cold and dry, and the SPAD was iced over and the motor refused to turn over.

'My artillerymen, little prepared for this sort of thing, and little assured, turned the prop without success. Then I asked them if they had any ether. There was some in their infirmary. I injected it into the cylinders by hand, made the compression in the same manner, and jumped into the cockpit to partially adjust the magneto for take-off – with success. In those days you had to know how to handle yourself in the wilderness.'

Flanked by his mechanics, Adjutant René Paul Louis Dousinelle of SPA48 poses beside his SPAD VII (No 12). Note that part of the wraparound windscreen has been removed, and a blue circle painted on to the centre section of the upper wing – an additional marking often seen on SPA48 aircraft. Dousinelle scored three victories in the SPAD VII between 21 September and 7 October 1917, and another six in SPAD XIIIs in 1918. He died on 28 January 1963 (*Daniel Porret via Jon Guttman*)

After some experimentation, the final production version of the SPAD VII solved the problem by developing an enlarged cowling with nine adjustable vertical shutters. From November 1916 on, the SPAD VII underwent some structural modifications as well, including simplified wire bracing inside the fuselage and the substitution of aluminium sockets for steel ones. The engine bearers were also reinforced with steel plates to reduce engine vibration.

Good though its performance was with the 150-hp Hispano-Suiza

engine, the SPAD VII's relatively heavy airframe rendered it less manoeuvrable than the Nieuport 17 it was meant to replace. The solution to this problem was to compensate with more power, and in late 1916 Marc Birkigt developed a more advanced version of his engine. The 8Ab, as it was called, had a compression ratio that had been increased from 4.7 to 5.3, raising its running speed from 1500 to 1800 rpm and its horsepower to 180, with a full-throttle capability of 204 hp.

SPAD VII S254 was the first example to be powered by the new engine, and it was of course presented to Guynemer in January 1917. By the end of the month his score had risen to 30, and he delightedly referred to the 180-hp SPAD as his *mitrailleuse volante* ('flying machine-gun'). He would score no less than 19 of his victories in S254 and, more significantly, its engine was never changed – a fact that speaks volumes for

Historic in at least two respects, S254 was the first SPAD VII equipped with the high-compression 180-hp Hispano-Suiza 8Ab engine, and was flown with considerable success by Lt Georges Guynemer. Painstakingly restored in the early 1980s, it is on display in the *Musée de l'Air et l'Espace* at Le Bourget, on the outskirts of Paris

An upper view of S254, showing the black leader's pennant on the fuselage upper decking and the 'mirror image' treatment of Guynemer's number '2' on the upper wing

both the reliability of the powerplant and the quality of SPA3's ground-crewmen, with whom Guynemer, who had himself been a mechanic before becoming a pilot, occasionally joined at their work.

Few aircraft could boast as many justifications for historic preservation as that first 180-hp SPAD, flown by France's most renowned fighter pilot. And indeed, after finally being retired from frontline service, S254 managed to survive the decades to be restored in the early 1980s and eventually displayed at the *Musée de l'Air et l'Espace* at Le Bourget.

Adjutant André Martenot de Cordoux, who was the first member of N94 to receive a SPAD VII, was another partisan of the 180-hp version, which became his favourite fighter. Born in Chalezeule on 14 March 1893, he had served with some distinction in the *149e Régiment d'Infanterie*, before transferring to aviation on 5 August 1915 and earning his pilot's brevet on 26 December.

While flying a Caudron G IV in C28, he and his gunner, Soldat 2ème Classe Claude Martin, downed an LVG on 20 May 1916. After further service in C56 and N38, Martenot was assigned to detachment N513, which was combined with detachments N512 and N514 to form *Escadrille* N94 on 1 June 1917. He scored his second victory (a Rumpler) while flying a Nieuport 24 on 25 July.

In September 1917 SPAD VII S135 was delivered to N94 and assigned to Martenot. Although he admitted that it was less manoeuvrable than the Nieuport 24, the future ace thought the SPAD nimble enough to hold its own against its German opponents in a dogfight if necessary. In a diving hit-and-run attack, he thought there were few aeroplanes comparable, thanks to the unsurpassed ability of its wing structure to hold up to the stress of a power dive. And even after Martenot had been issued a SPAD XIII (with double the armament and a 220-hp geared Hispano-Suiza 8B engine) in the spring of 1918, he chose to keep flying his old SPAD VII as well;

'I would fly regular missions in the SPAD XIII in order to keep formation, for the standard SPAD XIII was faster than the VII. When all the SPADs had returned, I would then use my VII between patrols on my own individual flights. Despite the single gun and lower speed, it was more manoeuvrable than the XIII and, frankly, the closeness of our combats rendered speed less important.

'My SPADs were originally fitted with the Aldis sight for aiming the gun or guns, but it presented a problem – it distorted distance, giving the impression that the target was closer than it was. I replaced the Aldis with a triple bead and "V" sight of my own invention, lining up my target with a set of cross-hairs without glass nearest my eye, a bead midway down the gun, and a "V" aperture near the muzzle. Because of this sight, my accuracy became so deadly that Germans seemed to avoid combat with me.'

Sgt André Henri Martenot de Cordoux glances at the camera from the cockpit of a SPAD VII. Martenot, who scored his first victory flying a Caudron G 4 with *Escadrille* C28, was the most experienced member of N94 when that unit was formed on 1 June 1917, and consequently received its first SPAD VII (S135) in July. He preferred the SPAD VII to the XIII, and flew both for a time, eventually being credited with eight victories

Martenot, who would be credited with seven or eight victories by the end of the war, stated that his fighting skills were largely refined during his brief stay in N38, where his mentor was that unit's leading ace, Adjutant Georges Félix Madon.

Born on 28 July 1892 in Bizerte, Tunisia, Madon had obtained a civil pilot's licence on 7 June 1911, and had been in the air service since 12 March 1912. He flew with Bl30 until 5 April 1915, when he became lost in bad weather and force-landed in neutral Switzerland. Interned, Madon made two attempts to escape, eventually succeeding on the second occasion (on 27 December). Returning to the front with MF218, he requested a transfer to a fighter squadron, and after training at Pau and Cazaux, he was assigned to N38 on 1 September 1916.

Although essentially attached to the *IVe Armée* to reconnoitre and photograph the frontline with camera-equipped Nieuports (which Martenot claimed to have done while he was there), N38 had a policy of aggressively defending its reconnaissance machines. Indeed, amongst its ranks were such aces as André Delorme (5 victories), Gustave Douchy (9), Jean Casale (13) and Hector Garaud (13).

Madon swiftly established himself as the most masterful of them all, claiming his first kill (a Fokker) on 28 September 1916. By 15 March 1917, when N38 was combined with N37, N78 and N112 to form GC15 under the command of Capitaine Victor Menard, Madon had claimed eight victories.

He downed his 16th opponent on 4 September, just as the first SPAD VIIs began supplanting the unit's Nieuports, and on 24 March 1918, now Lt Madon took command of SPA38 – by which time the unit had replaced its SPAD VIIs with XIIIs, and his score had risen to 25.

By the end of the war, Madon had been credited with 41 confirmed victories and 64 'probables'. The significant discrepancy between the two totals largely reflected an

Sgt Lionel de Marmier of SPA112 strikes a casual pose beside his SPAD VII in the autumn of 1917. Joining the unit on 1 December 1916, he failed to register a victory until 2 February 1918, when he and Sgt Reynaud downed a German two-seater south of Altkirch. He scored his sixth kill on 31 May, and was later credited with two or three victories in June 1940, while flying Caudron C 714s with Polish-manned GC1/145

Adjutant Hector Garaud proudly displays his decorations – the *Croix de Guerre* with five *Palmes* and two *Étoiles*, as well as the *Médaille Militaire*. Born in Saint-Antoine on 27 August 1897, he served in V97 before joining N38 on 16 April 1917. Flying the SPAD VII, he scored six victories in 1917, and brought his total up to 13 on 12 August 1918. Rising to the rank of commandant during World War 2, he fatally crashed during a test flight on 2 April 1940 (*via Greg VanWyngarden*)

SPAD VII S1415 was flown by SPA48's Cpl Jacques Raphaël Roques. Born in Paris to a Swiss father and a Venezuelan mother on 2 August 1897, Roques was a Swiss citizen who joined the Foreign Legion in order to transfer into the *Aviation Française*. He scored his second victory in this particular aeroplane, and three more in 1918, by which time he was flying SPAD XIIIs

attitude similar to René Dorme's – whenever Madon learned that a kill could not be confirmed by France's strict standards, he would dismiss the matter, remarking only that, 'The Boches know their losses'.

As it was, Madon was France's fourth-ranking ace, an *Officier de la Légion d'Honneur* and a recipient of the *Médaille Militaire* and *Croix de Guerre* with 17 *Palmes* and one *étoile de bronze*. Ironically, he was killed in a aeroplane crash in Tunis on 11 November 1924 while flying in a ceremony to commemorate the armistice, and the inauguration of a statue of pioneer aviator Roland Garros.

Martenot was but one of several French aces who regarded Madon as their mentor. Among them was SPA38's Hector Garaud, who was born in Saint-Antoine on 27 August 1897 and had served in V97 before joining the fighter unit on 16 April 1917.

He scored his first victory (flying a SPAD VII) on 12 May, and teamed up with Madon to bring down his sixth kill – a two-seater – over Tahure on 23 December. Awarded the *Médaille Militaire* on 2 January 1918, Garaud was promoted to adjutant on 20 February, and made a *Chevalier de la Légion d'Honneur* on 26 March, but on that same day he was wounded in the right lung while downing a Rumpler for his 12th victory. Garaud returned to combat in the summer and destroyed a Fokker D VII for his 13th victory on 12 August 1918, but he was wounded in the face by a shell splinter on 3 October. Commissioned a sous-lieutenant on 20 October, Garaud left the air service after the war to work in industry, but rejoined the reserve of the *Armée de l'Air* in 1932. Rising to the rank of Commandant during World War 2, he fatally crashed during a test flight on 2 April 1940.

Another of Madon's star pilots was Gustave Douchy, who started the war as an aeroplane mechanic, but completed his flight training on 15 July 1915 and was assigned to N38 on 24 October. He scored his first victories in the summer of 1916, added another seven to his tally between 22 January and 4 September 1917, and downed his ninth opponent on 6 March 1918.

According to Martenot, Madon at one time flew a SPAD with an all-red fuselage, while Douchy's machine was painted blue. On 26 March 1918, the latter ace was reassigned as a test pilot. During World War 2, he

served with the Free French forces after his country fell to the Germans, reaching the rank of capitaine on 1 February 1942. In June 1943, he was transferred from the Lebanon to Madagascar, where he was killed in an accident on 29 July. One other notable disciple of Madon's was American Cpl David Putnam, who scored five of his thirteen victories while serving in SPA38, and who is also alleged to have painted the fuselage of at least one of his SPADs red in emulation of Madon's practice.

While some French aces shared their fame with the units in which they served, others forfeited some notoriety by slowly but steadily accumulating victories in the course of several transfers from one unit to another.

A case in point was Edmond Jacques Marcel Pillon, who scored his first kill while flying a Voisin 3LA bomber in VB102 on 2 August 1916. On New Years' Day 1917, Pillon was assigned to newly-formed fighter *escadrille* N82, and he reopened his account by shooting down an enemy aeroplane over Verdun on 25 March 1917. His citation for the *Médaille Militaire* described how 'on 21 April 1917, he attacked a balloon which he forced to descend, and on 23 April he forced an enemy aeroplane to land behind the lines'. The latter victory – LVG C V 5155/17 – was Pillon's third, and the following day he downed Albatros D III 2120/16 near Altkirch, killing Vfw Rudolf Rath of Royal Bavarian *Jasta* 35.

N82 moved from the Lorraine sector to Matigny, six kilometres north-west of Ham, on 11 July, and shortly thereafter began receiving 180-hp SPAD VIIs to supplement its Nieuports. Pillon was assigned one, and he used it to attack three German balloons on 19 and 20 August. On 31 August, the SPAD's ruggedness again served him well when he strafed the German trenches at low altitude.

At 1655 hrs on 3 September, he spotted four German scouts patrolling over one of their balloons. Diving into the middle of the flight, Pillon picked out the leader and sent him down north-west of Laon before the other three attacked him. The ace managed to fight his way back to French lines with his fuel almost spent – he had also downed a two-seater during this mission. Exactly one week later he was wounded, but returned to combat with SPA67 on 15 April 1918. Pillon would score two more victories with this unit, and his eighth with SPA98 on 2 September 1918.

Pillon was killed in a crash at the Farman aerodrome at Toussus-le-Noble on 8 June 1921 – just a day before his 30th birthday.

While most French *escadrilles* used numerals for individual identification, SPA23 chose to mark its SPAD VIIs with a red stripe, applied along the fuselage side and across the upper wing. Note also the individual motifs for the pilots, none of whom can be positively linked to either of these machines (*SHAA B76.1853 via Jon Guttman*)

SOLDIERING ON INTO 1918

Delays in SPAD XIII production, combined with problems with the newer type's geared engine, resulted in the SPAD VII remaining in service longer than expected. When the Germans launched their spring offensive on 21 March 1918, the Allies needed every aeroplane they could muster, and although the SPAD XIII was available in quantity, the SPAD VII's proven reliability kept it a vital asset to France's fighter force. On 1 April 1918, there were still 372 SPAD VIIs at the front, outnumbering the 290 available SPAD XIIIs.

Among a number of pilots still achieving success with the older SPAD during the spring of 1918 was one of France's pioneer aces. Born in Paris on 17 September 1893, Jean Chaput had entered military service in 1913, and was in the *36ème Régiment d'Infanterie* when war broke out. Transferring to aviation soon after, he opened his account with a Fokker *Eindecker* on 12 June 1915 while flying a Caudron G IV with C28. Scoring two more victories in the *Groupement d'Angers*, before joining N57 on 7 May 1916, Chaput subsequently saw much action in Morane-Saulnier N monoplanes and Nieuports, and had increased his tally to eight victories by the end of 1916.

Following his unit's re-equipment with SPADs, he scored his first victories with the new type on 5 April 1917 when he claimed two kills. By 21 April 1918, Chaput was credited with a total of 16 enemy aeroplanes

SPA48's Lt Armand de Turenne stands beside his SPAD VII, which is decorated with the large cockerel's head emblem that he helped design for the *escadrille*. Joining N48 on 14 June 1916, Turenne scored six kills with the unit before being made CO of SPA12 on 12 January 1918, and bringing his total up to 15

SPA57's Sous-Lt Jean Chaput poses by the wing of his SPAD VII in the late summer of 1917. Born in Paris on 17 September 1893, Chaput opened his account with an *Eindecker* on 12 June 1915 while flying a Caudron G 4 with C28. He saw further action in Morane-Saulnier monoplanes, Nieuports and SPADs, downing some 16 aircraft. Chaput's luck finally ran out on 6 May, when he was mortally wounded in the femoral artery during a fight with Fokker Dr Is of *Jasta* 12. His victor was the unit's commander, Ltn Hermann Becker

destroyed, including that of ten-victory ace Ltn Erich Thomas of *Jasta* 22, who was taken prisoner on 23 March 1918.

Chaput was made commander of SPA57 on 11 April 1918, and one of his first acts was to replace the wild boar emblem that had charged along the fuselage sides of its SPADs in 1917 – and which few of its pilots had really liked – with his personal seagull marking as a unit insignia. Chaput's tenure as CO was destined to last less than a month, however. During a dogfight with Fokker Dr Is on 6 May 1918, he was struck in the femoral artery, and although he managed to bring his SPAD VII (S4280) in for a crash-landing, he bled to death before he could be hospitalised. Chaput's demise was credited to Leutnant der Reserve Hermann Becker, commander of *Jasta* 12.

An almost parallel career to Chaput's was that of Omer Paul Demeuldre, who was born in Cambrai on 8 March 1892 and who entered the military in 1912. Soon after war broke out, he was assigned to MF63 as a mechanic, although he was serving as the machine-gunner of one of the *escadrille's* Maurice Farmans, with Sgt Teulon as his pilot, when he shot down an Albatros two-seater over Bois de Forges on 7 September 1915.

After being sent for pilot training and receiving his military pilot's brevet on 2 October 1916, Demeuldre rejoined his old unit. *Escadrille* 63 was subsequently re-equipped with Sopwith 1.A2s (licence-built 1½ Strutters), and he was piloting one of these when he and his observer, Sgt Lemarc, downed an enemy scout on 23 May 1917. In October, the aggressive Demeuldre was transferred to SPA84, and he was flying a SPAD VII on the 30th when he sent an enemy aeroplane down in flames near Aboddage. This, his third victory, also brought him a citation for the *Médaille Militaire.*

Demeuldre added an Albatros to his score on 15 December, followed by a DFW C V on 22 December and another the next day. He started 1918 with an enemy aeroplane destroyed on 3 January, and on the 25th he received a sous-lieutenant's commission. Two more aircraft fell to him

Sous-Lt Marius Hasdenteufel (far left) of SPA57 is congratulated by senior officers upon his return from a successful sortie – probably the one in which he scored his fifth victory, in concert with Sous-Lt Charles Nuville. Their victim was Ltn Kurt Schulz of *Jasta* 37, who was killed when his Fokker D VII crashed in flames south of Dormans on 25 June 1918. Newly-crowned ace Hasdenteufel was killed in an accident the very next day. His de Marçay-built SPAD VII is marked with a seagull, which was originally devised by Lt Jean Chaput as a personal marking. It was duly adopted by SPA57 as the unit insignia in place of the boar – which nobody in the *escadrille* really liked – when Chaput assumed command on 11 April 1918 (*SHAA B84.1702 via Jon Guttman*)

Sous-Lt Georges Jacques Toussaint François Ortoli, visiting SPA57 from neighbouring SPA31, poses alongside Chaput's SPAD VII. Born on 16 July 1895 in Puggio de Tallano, Corsica, Ortoli scored his first victory on 28 April 1915 in an MF8 Maurice Farman, with Lt Jules Menj as his observer. Later, whilst flying fighters in N31, he increased his total to 11. Promoted to lieutenant on 19 April 1918, he commanded SPA57 from 10 May to the end of the war. Ortoli returned to military service during World War 2, retired on 15 July 1945 and died in Tunis, Tunisia, on 19 March 1947

Adjutant Pierre Pendaries of SPA69 prepares to take off in his SPAD, *"MOUSTIC V"* (a slang reference to a mosquito). After being wounded as an infantryman on 17 December 1914, Pendaries transferred to aviation and was assigned to N69, scoring his first victory on 1 August 1916. He downed two more enemy aircraft on 22 April and 3 May 1917, and four or five more in 1918

on 3 February, after which he downed a Rumpler two-seater on 8 March, and shot the wings off another on the 16th. Demeuldre teamed up with squadronmates to down an enemy aeroplane on 23 March and a two-seater on 14 April, increasing his tally to 13 confirmed and 12 'probables'.

While flying his third patrol of the day on 3 May 1918, Demeuldre encountered an enemy two-seater over Montdidier and attacked it at close range – only to be struck first by the German observer. Demeuldre fell to his death near Champagne Pouilleuse, and he was posthumously made a *Chevalier de la Légion d'Honneur.*

While Chaput's and Demeuldre's fighting careers were ending in the cockpits of SPAD VIIs in May 1918, that of Adjutant Arthur Marie Marcel Coadou was just beginning. Born in St Brieuc on 7 February 1894, Coadou had initially served in C59, before being reassigned to N88 on 25 January 1917.

Over the next year, Coadou established a reputation as a steady team player, with a cautious approach to combat that some of his squadronmates thought a bit excessive, and which earned him the nickname of *'Judex'* (a slang contraction of *judicieux*). Coadou was enough of a 'sport' to apply the nickname to the side of his fighters, but it took on an ironic meaning when he finally shot down an enemy aeroplane while flying a SPAD VII on 19 May 1918. From that point onwards, *'Judex'* became more aggressive, claiming fifteen victories – nine of which were confirmed – by the end of the war (albeit mostly in SPAD XIIIs).

Another SPAD VII champion during the German spring offensive of

1918 was the highest-scoring Swiss ace of the war. Born in Esmans (Seine-et-Marne) on 1 June 1894 of Swiss parents, Sgt André Louis Bosson enlisted in the French army on 6 September 1914, and transferred to the air service in 1917 – he was the only non-French citizen to enter service without joining the Foreign Legion.

Joining SPA62 on Christmas Eve 1917, Bosson scored his first confirmed victory on 9 March, and his second three days later. After more than two months of ground attack and reconnaissance missions, he resumed his aerial exploits with a vengeance with a two-seater on 27 May, another the following day and an Albatros on 30 May. A second Albatros fell to Bosson's gun on 2 June, and he and Sous-Lt Jean-Paul Jacques Favre de Thierrens shared in shooting down an Albatros D V over Soissons on 4 June. That brought Bosson's score up to seven and Favre de Thierrens' to six, but on 20 July Bosson was mortally wounded by German ground fire east of Hartennes whilst flying de Marçay-built SPAD VII S5325.

In addition to the multitude of fighter *escadrilles* operating SPAD VIIs over the Western Front, the type also served with N531 in Salonika, N561 in Venice and N581 in Russia.

Formed on 13 March 1918, N531 was made up of French and Greek personnel, under a Greek CO. One of its French members, Adjutant-Chef Dieudonné Costes, may have used a SPAD VII to score

Born on 20 June 1894, Sous-Lt William Herisson scored 11 victories with SPA75, his last being a 'double' when he and two squadronmates downed a German two-seater and a Fokker D VII on 17 September 1918. He died on Christmas Day 1969 in the town of his birth, Nîmes

A former artilleryman, Lt Jean-Paul Jacques Favre de Thierrens served with F215 until wounded by shrapnel on 2 September 1916, then returned to combat with N62. The later *escadrille* was a fighter-reconnaissance unit attached to the *VI Armée* which produced no less than six aces. Favre de Thierrens scored six victories with the squadron, was made a *Chevalier de la Légion d'Honneur* and attained the rank of lieutenant-colonel during World War 2. He died in Paris on 17 October 1973, aged 78

some of the four victories he claimed with the unit (out of a grand total of eight). He later went on to even greater renown on 1-2 September 1930 when he and Maurice Bellonte flew the Atlantic Ocean from east to west non-stop in a modified Bréguet XIX, covering 6500 kilometres in 37 hours and 17 minutes. Fellow N531 pilot Sgt Basile Félicien Saune downed five enemy aircraft between 30 April and 13 June 1918. Promoted to adjutant on 2 May, and commissioned a sous-lieutenant on 19 June, Saune was killed in combat with several German aircraft while flying SPAD VII S5790 the very next day. He had fallen victim to Leutnant der Reserve Gerhard Fieseler of *Jasta* 25.

As late as September 1918, the newly-formed SPA167 had twelve SPAD XIIIs and six SPAD VIIs on strength. Eventually, some 3500 SPAD VIIs were built, and these served with numerous air arms across the globe both during and after World War 1 – including in France, where fledgling fighter pilots were using them for training as late as 1928.

BALLOON BUSTING

Captive or kite balloons, also known as *Drachen* ('dragons' – an Austrian analogy for Chinese kites) and 'Sausages', were the oldest form of aerial reconnaissance, having first been used by the French in 1795. They saw considerable use during World War 1, for they could stay in the air longer than aeroplanes and, thanks to their stabilising fins, provided the observer with a steady platform from which to scan large chunks of the frontline.

Communicating by telephone with forces on the ground, the balloon observers could direct artillery or detect frontline movements, and as such, constituted a very real menace to the other side's troops. Destroying enemy balloons, therefore, was a very desirable objective before a major offensive, defensive or logistic support operation could be carried out.

On the face of it, a large bag of hydrogen would seem an easy target for an enterprising fighter pilot, but most airmen regarded balloon-busting missions as extraordinarily difficult and dangerous. The balloons were located deep within enemy territory, requiring their attackers to go after them, thus exposing the attackers to anti-aircraft fire, enemy fighters and every enemy soldier carrying a gun.

Rigged for a balloon-busting mission, this SPAD VII of SPA103 has tubes for Le Prieur rockets attached to the inner set of interplane struts. Impressive but inaccurate, the rockets seldom succeeded in destroying their intended targets (*SHAAB83.4994 via Jon Guttman*)

High-scoring ace Capitaine Charles Nungesser (left) of SPA65 visits SPA88's CO, Lt Gabriel Fernand Charles Guérin, in July 1918. The latter pilot downed 22 opponents with SPA15 before being wounded on 11 May 1918. Upon his recovery, Guérin was given command of SPA88 on 7 July, and he claimed his 23rd victory on 19 July . . .

. . . but less than a fortnight later he was dead. On 1 August 1918, Lt Guérin was taking off on a patrol from SPA88's aerodrome at Mont-l'Eveque when his SPAD VII suddenly spun into the ground and he was killed

Although the balloon floated several thousand feet above the ground, it could be rapidly brought down by means of a powered winch when attacked, while a cordon of anti-aircraft guns surrounded it with a descending cone of fire through which the attacking fighter had to dive.

Once he reached the balloon, the fighter pilot found it surprisingly difficult to ignite pure hydrogen, even with incendiary bullets. Only by pouring a sustained burst into the gas bag, allowing some hydrogen to escape and mix with the oxygen, could the attacker hope to create the fire that, once started, would quickly consume the entire balloon.

Once ignited, a burning balloon could be seen for miles, assuring confirmation for the fighter pilot who destroyed it – provided he returned to claim the kill. But the pyre was equally visible to the enemy, and the balloon buster faced a gauntlet of anti-aircraft and ground fire, as well as vengeful enemy fighters converging on his most likely escape route.

Taken in sum, these factors rendered balloon busting a suicide mission, requiring as much luck as skill on the pilot's part, and an aeroplane capable of standing up to considerable punishment. French ace of aces René Fonck, who hated leaving anything to chance, did not include a single balloon among his 75 victories, stating in no uncertain terms that 'I do not thus like to combat the enemy, and I prefer to leave it to the specialists of such attacks'. The few airmen who made a practice of volunteering for anti-*Drachen* missions were regarded as something of a special breed, possessed of a combination of pyromania and a latent death wish known as 'balloon fever'.

Almost as rare as the balloon specialists were the aircraft fast and sturdy enough to improve the odds of carrying out the mission and returning to boast of it. Among that robust few were the British SE 5a, the German Pfalz D III and the French SPAD VII. Possessing a proven ability to stand up to stress and punishment, the SPAD VII was limited only by its single machine gun, which was usually armed with special ammunition, such as a mix of flat-nosed Buckingham bullets to tear the balloon and incendiary rounds to ignite the escaping hydrogen as it mixed with the air.

By mid-1917, some SPAD VIIs were also equipped with Le Prieur rockets, fired from six to eight tubes mounted on the inner set of inter-plane struts. Although Le Prieur rocket attacks made a spectacular show,

A formal portrait of Adjutant Pierre de Cazenove de Pradines of SPA81, who survived being shot down by Ltn Ernst Udet on 20 February 1917, and went on to destroy four German aircraft and one balloon in the SPAD VII. Badly wounded in the knee on December 1917, he returned to SPA81 in 1918 and scored a further two victories in SPAD XIIIs

Sous-Lt André Herbelin's SPAD VII displays a personal variation on the grim reaper theme, along with the legend *RISQUE TOUT* (daredevil) and the diagonal red-white-red wing stripes that served as SPA81's squadron marking for most of 1917. Later, when SPA81 adopted a greyhound as its insignia, Herbelin added a white rabbit with a Maltese cross running in front of his canine emblem. Scoring 11 victories in World War 1, Herbelin later fought with the French Resistance in World War 2, and retired as a lieutenant-colonel and a *Commandant de la Légion d'Honneur*. He died on 16 December 1966, aged 77 (*via Philippe Lagnier*)

they were wildly inaccurate, and seldom effective even at close range.

One French ace who had a go with the rockets was Adjutant Pierre de Cazenove de Pradines, the scion of a long line of career officers who had begun his military career in the *14e Régiment des Houzards*. 'Ultimately I spent most of my soldiering off my horse and in the trenches', he remarked. 'I could not take this and so I decided to enter aviation in March 1916'.

In December 1916 he joined *Escadrille* N81, then equipped with Nieuport 17s, which was the type he was flying on 20 February 1917 when he was forced down in no-man's-land by two Albatros D IIIs and subsequently credited to *Jasta* 15's Ltn Ernst Udet as his fourth victory.

Cazenove later flew a SPAD VII bearing the twin sets of diagonal red-white-red stripes across the upper wing that served as SPA81's first unit marking. He combined this with his old cavalry unit's colours in the form of a sky-blue diagonal band on the fuselage as a personal marking.

In a similarly equestrian vein, Cazenove's squadronmate, Sous-Lt Jacques Leps, marked the right side of his fighter's fuselage with the word *L'HOUZARD* (an archaic spelling of *hussard*) and the left side with the name *BERCHENY*, which was a reference to the Hungarian founder of the Bercheny Hussars during the 18th century reign of King Louis XV. During the Napoleonic era the regiment had been redesignated the 1st Hussars, and Leps had served with the unit prior to transferring to the air service.

On 26 May, Cazenove sent an Albatros scout down trailing smoke following an engagement over Reims – this was his first victory. On 19 August, he flew his first, and only, balloon mission using the rockets, which he later described;

'On 20 August 1917 the Third Battle of Verdun began. In the days preceding that battle, it was vital that all enemy balloons be eliminated from the sky. One day Capitaine Raymond Bailly (SPA81's commander) asked for one pilot to volunteer to destroy one balloon (at Montfaucon). I put myself forward and started preparing for the sortie. Arming my SPAD with Le Prieur rockets mounted on the wing struts – an electric charge set them off – I soon found my quarry and dived fast as the machine gun batteries opened up.

'At the right moment I pulled up and the rockets fired off in all directions in an impressive smoky display. When it cleared, I found myself heading for an intact balloon – the rockets had gone in every direction except at the target! I withdrew, with only one bullet through my aeroplane, but on my way back home I was approached by another machine. As it closed, I was relieved to see the name *BERCHENY* on the side of the fuselage – Leps! He escorted me home.

'The next day (20 August) I returned with phosphorus bullets in my machine gun and flamed that balloon. In the same afternoon the Chief of Combat Aviation flew over from Headquarters to our field to confer upon me the *Médaille Militaire* before any recommendation.'

Cazenove's score stood at five when he attacked a two-seater on 9 December, only to be struck in the leg by the German gunner, 'breaking the tibia just below the kneecap and shattering the leg bone', as he described it. He managed to land near a hospital at Verdun Faubourg de Glorieux, on the verge of fainting from loss of blood. His leg was not amputated, but when he rejoined SPA81 five months later, he said, 'I was greatly troubled by the vibrations of my aeroplane. I had my mechanic rig an elastic support for my left leg, which I used when taking off, and which

Adjutant de Cazenove (left) and Adjutant-Chef Henri Peronneau (middle) discuss their latest combat with Lt William Thaw of N124 *Lafayette* amid the wreckage of a Halberstadt CL II that the Frenchmen had jointly shot down on 22 September 1917. Entering the Aviation Service in Western Morocco in 1912, Peronneau had seen action with N49 and N65 prior to transferring to N81 on Boxing Day 1916. The victory of 22 September was his first of an eventual nine, the last two of which were also two-seaters shared with de Cazenove, on 1 and 31 July 1918. Peronneau died in Tunisia on 10 August 1960, six days after his 70th birthday

Members of SPA81 pose for a group shot between patrols. They are, from left to right, Adjutants Henri Peronneau and Paul Guérin and Lts Adrien Louis Jacques Leps, Marcel Dhôme and Levecque. A St-Cyr graduate, Jacques Leps transferred from the *9e* to the *1e Régiment de Hussards* on 4 November 1914. Transferring to SPA81 on 14 December 1916, his early SPAD VIIs bore a reference to the *1e Hussards'* pre-Napoleonic Era name on both sides of the fuselage – *L'HOUZARD* on the right and *BERCHENY* on the left. Leps was placed in command of SPA81 on 24 February 1918, and he survived the war with 12 victories to his credit. He served as a commandant in GC21 during World War 2, and eventually retired as a lieutenant-colonel and *Commandeur de la Légion d'Honneur*

SPAD VII S3158 of SPA81 is seen in typical 1918 camouflage, sporting a red cowling and the final version of the unit's greyhound emblem. The latter motif, according to Pierre Cardon, was designed by *Lafayette* Flying Corps volunteer Alexander Bayne, who had created a stencil to facilitate its easy application on all the unit's scouts

relieved me a lot. Despite this handicap, I downed two more enemy aircraft'.

All five of fellow SPA81 ace Pierre Cardon's victories were scored against balloons, and he claimed them all while flying a SPAD VII. Like Cazenove, he found balloon busting both exhilarating and terrifying.

The son of an industrialist from Armentiéres, Pierre Marie Joseph Cardon was studying engineering at the *Institute Catholique des Artes et Métiers* at Lille when war broke out in August 1914, at which point he and his younger brother, Michel, joined the *5e Régiment des Chasseur á Cheval.* They were soon off their horses and in the trenches, however, leading Pierre to request a transfer to *Escadrille* C64 as a mechanic.

In January 1917, both he and his brother managed to enter the pilots' school at Avord, obtaining their flying Brevets in Caudron G IIIs in April. Both became instructors, Pierre's students including future American ace Frank Baylies and a Pole in the Imperial Russian Air Service, Stefan Pawlikowski, who went on to fly in SPA96 and would later be commander

Although SPA65's most famous ace was Charles Nungesser, the unit produced other successful pilots such as Sgt Jacques Gerard, who is seen here standing beside his SPAD VII. This snowy shot was almost certainly taken soon after he had scored his first victory, in concert with Sous-Lt André Borde, on 30 January 1918. Gerard was awarded the *Médaille Militaire* after downing two enemy two-seaters on 23 April, and he destroyed his eighth opponent on 28 June. Gerard was eventually killed in action on 3 July 1918 (*SHAA B76.1809 via Jon Guttman*)

of the Polish Air Force's fighter arm during World War 2.

Following Michel Cardon's death in a flying accident on 10 September 1917, Pierre asked to return to the front as a fighter pilot and after training at Avord, Pau (home of the acrobatic school) and Cazeaux (the gunnery training centre), he joined SPA81 at Beauzée on 15 December 1917.

Although the unit was largely equipped with SPAD XIIIs, Sgt Cardon flew all his missions in an older SPAD VII. He was wounded on 5 April 1918, when he returned to base

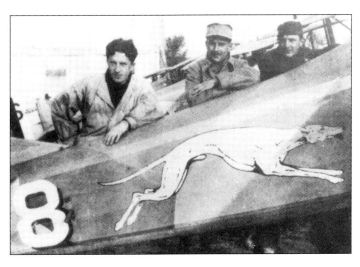

Sgt Pierre Cardon leans on the fuselage of his SPAD VII in May 1918, flanked by his mechanics, Charles Boillot (left) and Charrière. After the death of his brother, Michel, in an air accident, Pierre Cardon requested fighter training, and on 15 December 1917 he joined SPA81. He was duly credited with sharing in the destruction of five balloons, the last of which he flew through as it exploded in flames

with 18 bullet holes in his fighter. He came into his stride on 15 May, however, when he burned a *Drachen* in collaboration with his commander, Lt Leps, during a sweep to eliminate German kite balloons from the area. He then teamed up with Maréchal-des-Logis Louis Chaigneau to destroy another, the latter pilot also flaming a third gas bag on his own.

On 31 May Cardon, now promoted to maréchal-des-logis, shared in the destruction of a third balloon with Sgt Maurice Rousselle, and three days later he, Adjutant Alphonse Malfanti and Sgt Paul Guérin burned yet another. Cardon later commented;

'Among the persons cited in collaboration, Chaigneau, Rousselle and myself possessed incendiary machine gun bullets specifically for the balloons. The other participants had only ordinary machine guns. I never took a bullet in my aeroplane in any of my balloon attacks.'

Cardon's final victory was also his most memorable. On 6 June, he accompanied Leps and Rousselle on another 'sausage roast', and they duly found a balloon north-west of Soissons. Attacking together, Cardon described what happened next;

'We were all so intent on the *Drachen* that it was only at the last moment I looked around and saw that Leps and Rousselle were converging on me! I took evasive measures, with the result that we did not collide, but I went through the flames and smoke of the exploding balloon. I emerged with my carburettor full of gum and burnt rubber. The rubbery stuff choked the engine, and I had to glide in. My aeroplane was in a pitiful state, but I managed to reach our side of the lines.'

So ended Cardon's three-week 'scoring streak'. Although he served faithfully in SPA81 to the end of the war, he added no more confirmed victories to his tally.

Several French 'balloon busters' achieved some of their successes in the SPAD VII, including François Guerrier of SPA77 (five balloons), Paul Santelli of SPA81 (seven balloons), Claude Haegelen of SPA100 (12 balloons in a total of 22 victories), Maurice Boyau of SPA77 (21 balloons in a total of 35 victories) and Léon Jean-Pierre Bourjade of SPA152 (27 ballons in a total of 28 victories).

The most effective anti-*Drachen* unit was SPA154, led by Lt Michel Coiffard, who claimed 24 balloons out of a total of 34 victories. Other

SPA81's five-victory ace Sgt Paul Santelli (right) gives a lively lecture on tactics for his squadronmates. They are, (standing) from left to right, Adjutants Alphonse Malphanti (four victories) and Léon Blanc, Sgt Colanbo and Adjutant Maurice Rousselle (five victories), while Sgt Pierre Cardon is seated in front

balloon aces within the *escadrille* were Jacques Ehrlich (18 balloons out of 19 victories), Henri Condemine (nine victories, all of which were balloons), Paul Barbreau (eight, all of which were balloons), Paul Yvan Robert Waddington (five balloons out of twelve victories), Louis Gros (five balloons out of nine victories), Auguste Lahoulle (four balloons out of ten victories), Paul Armand Petit (four balloons out of seven victories) and Xavier Moissinac (one balloon out of seven victories).

These aces scored the majority of their victories in mid-to-late 1918 while flying SPAD XIIIs, however, for the newer type boasted greater firepower thanks to its twin Vickers machine guns.

SPADs Under the Iron Cross

Many rumours circulated among Allied airmen of the 'Dastardly Hun' employing captured aircraft in combat during World War 1. Most such reports were as apocryphal as the more grotesque stories of German atrocities in Belgium, although like most exaggerations they were based on a kernel of truth. At least two SPAD VIIs are known to have been flown by German aces, although it is doubtful that they flew them over the frontlines more than once, if at all.

The best-known case was that of Oblt Eduard Ritter von Schleich, the Bavarian leader of *Jasta* 21 (and eventual 35-victory ace and *Pour le Mérite* recipient) who went up in a captured SPAD, and could not resist flying it over Allied territory. For further amusement, he joining a French formation just to see how long it would take them to notice the black crosses on his machine. According to the account, the French soon did, but Schleich escaped by diving away – only to come under intense fire as he returned over the frontlines from German troops who were better at identifying the silhouette of a SPAD VII than they were at noting the crosses on his wings! After a dressing-down by his superiors, Schleich retired his SPAD and returned to flying Albatros D Vs.

Oberleutnant Eduard Ritter von Schleich of *Jasta* 21 poses beside a SPAD VII of SPA65. This aircraft was almost certainly the mount of *Lafayette* Flying Corps member Sgt Everett T Buckley, who was brought down by Ltn Otto Kissenberth of neighbouring *Jasta* 23 on 6 September 1917. This may also have been the machine that Schleich flew over Allied territory in a prank that almost got him shot down – by his own troops!

Schleich was indeed photographed beside a SPAD VII bearing the dragon insignia of SPA65, with Albatros D Vs of *Jasta* 21 in the background, the setting for this shot most likely being the aerodrome at Chassogne, near Verdun. Schleich was not credited with having downed any of SPA65's SPADs, although his friend, and fellow Bavarian, Ltn Otto Kissenberth, who was CO of neighbouring *Jasta* 23, was – on 6 September 1917 he downed the SPAD VII of Sgt Everett T Buckley, an American of the LFC who was taken prisoner (and who, after several attempts, eventually escaped). Schleich was probably 'borrowing' Buckley's SPAD when he flew his less-than-auspicious prank sortie over the lines.

Coincidentally, at least one other SPA65 SPAD VII was associated with a German ace. Bearing a somewhat different variation of the *escadrille's* dragon emblem as worn on Buckley's scout, it was photographed on a snowy aerodrome with Leutnant der Reserve Rudolf Windisch, commander of the newly formed *Jasta* 66, in the cockpit.

On 12 January 1918, Sgt Joseph Leboucher was brought down and taken prisoner in SPAD S4267, probably by Ltn Fritz Pütter of *Jasta* 9 – again, a *Staffel* based in the same sector as *Jasta* 66. The SPAD was repainted in a dark colour (probably black), with the dragon emblem retained, along with a border of what was probably the original light yellow finish. Also retained were the tricolour bands on the upper wing, while partial bands of red and white graced the fuselage upper decking.

Whether Windisch actually flew the SPAD in combat is unknown and, given Schleich's experience in it the previous autumn, it seems highly unlikely. One of the first German pilots to fly the new Fokker D VII, Windisch had increased his score to 22 by the time he was brought down on 27 May 1918 by two SPAD pilots, Sous-Lt Souleau and Maréc hal-des-Logis Hyppolyte Cavieux of SPA76. Subsequent reports stated variously that the ace was taken prisoner and that he had then been killed – perhaps while trying to escape?

S4267 was yet another SPA65 SPAD VII that fell into enemy hands in one piece. Flown by Sgt Joseph Leboucher, it was brought down on 12 January 1918 by Ltn Fritz Pütter of *Jasta* 9 and the pilot captured. Overpainted in a dark colour (possibly black?), the SPAD was flown by Leutnant der Reserve Rudolf Windisch of *Jasta* 66, although it is not known whether he used it for purposes other than evaluation

SPADS FOR THE RFC

Britain was swift to see the SPAD VII's worth as a fighter, but relatively slow to get it into frontline service. Three SPADs were initially made available for service evaluation with No 60 Sqn in September 1916, with one of them, S126, being given the British serial number A.253. It was duly flown by Capt Ernest Leslie Foot, one of the RFC's 'old guard'.

SPAD VII S126 is shown shortly after its arrival at No 2 Aircraft Depot, Candas, on 9 September 1916 – note that its Royal Flying Corps serial A.253 has been somewhat crudely applied. A blue-white-red cockade was later added to the fuselage side, and on 20 September the machine was assigned to No 60 Sqn for evaluation. On 28 September it became the first British SPAD to achieve success when Capt Ernest L Foot destroyed an Albatros two-seater over Avesnes les Bapaume for his fourth victory (*via Leslie Rogers*)

'Feet' Foot had flown FE 2bs with No 11 Sqn, and was a close friend of a squadronmate who went on to greater fame with No 60 Sqn – Albert Ball. A day after scoring his third kill on 15 September, Foot was posted to No 60 Sqn, where he gave the British SPAD its baptism of fire on 28 September, when he attacked four Albatros two-seaters and downed one of them near Avesnes les Bapaume.

Foot went on to 'make ace' while flying one of No 60 Sqn's standard complement of Nieuports on 21 October, although five days later he was shot down by Ltn Hans Imelmann of *Jasta* 2. Emerging uninjured from his crash-landing, he was posted home for a rest on 3 November.

Like his friend Ball, Foot was next slated to serve as a flight leader in No 56 Sqn on 10 March 1917, but he was injured in a car accident the evening before the newly-formed unit was to leave for France, which ended his wartime flying. Foot was subsequently killed when the civilian Bristol M 1D monoplane he was flying lost a wing and crashed near Chertsey on 23 June 1923.

On 30 September 1916, the commander of the RFC, Maj-Gen Hugh M Trenchard, asked for 30 more SPADs, and on 5 October the French Ministry of War authorised the purchase of these airframes, with the understanding that the British would supply the engines. That same month No 19 Sqn began replacing its BE 12s with SPADs, although the unit would not be completely re-equipped until February 1917.

SPAD VII A.6706 displays the dumb-bell marking that appeared at various times on aircraft of No 19 Sqn – in this case on 24 March 1917, when the aeroplane was brought down and its pilot, Lt Richard P Baker, wounded and taken prisoner. Baker was victory No 30 for *Jasta* 11's commander, Oblt Manfred Freiherr von Richthofen (*via Leslie Rogers*)

Meanwhile, arrangements had been made for licence production of the SPAD VII in the UK by Mann, Egerton & Co Ltd of Norwich and L Blériot (Aeronautics) at Brooklands, which later changed its name to Blériot & SPAD and moved to Addlestone. In December 1916 the Admiralty ordered 50 SPADs from British Nieuport for the Royal Naval Air Service, but in February 1917 that order was changed to SE 5s and then, on 5 March, to Nieuport scouts. Relatively few British-built SPADs reached the Western Front, with most of those serving with Nos 19 and 23 Sqns being French-built aircraft. Another 19 SPAD VIIs were allocated to Nos 30, 63 and 72 Sqns in the Middle East.

Coincident with the completion of No 19 Sqn's transition to the SPAD VII came a new commander, Maj Hubert D Harvey-Kelly, in February 1917. The first British pilot to arrive on French soil following the outbreak of war (in a BE 2a of No 2 Sqn on 13 August 1914), Harvey-Kelly was also credited with the RFC's first air-to-air victory when he attacked a German Taube with his pistol on 25 August. Compelling its crew to land and flee into the woods, he then landed alongside the machine and set it alight, before taking off once again!

Following familiarisation flights at St Omer and gunnery training at Camiers, Harvey-Kelly moved his unit to Vert Galant, and commenced operations in March 1917. On the 17th of that month he reported;

'At about 1030 hrs I was at 13,000 ft when I saw a large two-seater, and an Albatros scout about 4000 ft above him. I made for the two-seater and gave him a burst at long range and then climbed quickly and got above the scout. The scout turned east with engine on and slightly nose down. The SPAD, however, quickly caught him. I opened fire about 200 ft above him. A jam occurred after the first round and the engagement was broken off. The jam was cleared and the gun fired satisfactorily.

'At about 1110 hrs I saw another Albatros scout above me. On manoeuvring for position, the SPAD easily outclimbed the Albatros, which then dived away. The SPAD followed and opened fire at about 150 ft (and) jammed after the first round. This jam could not be freed in the air and machine returned on this account.'

Harvey-Kelly's experience showed that the SPAD VII could hold its own against the best the Germans had, if only its Vickers gun could be kept from jamming. Three pilots went missing in March, while Lt Augustus H Orlebar claimed a Halberstadt D II that could not be confirmed on 24 March. Lt G S Buck officially opened the SPAD squadron's account with an Albatros scout out of control near Brebiéres on 13 April, and by the end of the month three more kills had been claimed. These included an Albatros two-seater by Lt James Martin Child on 23 April and an Albatros scout by Harvey-Kelly the following day.

The new SPADs, however, were now up against the most skilled and experienced airmen in the *Luftstreitkräfte*, and No 19 Sqn would suffer its share of casualties amid the aerial debacle known as 'Bloody April', with five fighters and their pilots lost, and a further two men wounded. The worst day was 29 April 1917, when two flights were sent up and, when a third was called for by Wing Headquarters, Harvey-Kelly led his two remaining pilots, Lt W N Hamilton and 2Lt Richard Applin, on a mission to Douai. On the way, they encountered three red-coloured Albatros D IIIs and five silvery-grey D IIIs.

Capt Augustus Henry Orlebar scored his first two victories in SPAD A.6663 with No 19 Sqn, four more flying Sopwith Camels with No 73 Sqn (including the Fokker Dr I of Ltn Lothar von Richthofen of *Jasta* 11 on 13 March 1918) and his seventh in a Sopwith Snipe with No 43 Sqn on 29 September 1918. He is shown here serving as a captain with the latter unit (*via Norman Franks*)

SPAD B'3508 of No 19 Sqn had a light band and a dark letter 'C' applied to its rear fuselage. On 25 September 1917, 2Lt R G Holt used this machine to destroy a German two-seater south-east of Gheluvelt, but it was in turn brought down on 6 October and its pilot, Lt G R Long, taken prisoner (*via Leslie Rogers*)

Harvey-Kelly noticed six Sopwith Triplanes of No 1 Sqn RNAS nearby, and figuring that they would join in, he attacked the three red machines. The Triplanes did indeed enter the fray, claiming three Albatros scouts out of control in a 20-minute dogfight, but Harvey-Kelly's SPADs could scarcely have squared off with a more formidable trio, for their crimson opponents were from *Jasta* 11, led by Hptm Manfred Freiherr von Richthofen. The British would have been somewhat flattered, however, had they read Richthofen's account of the fight afterward, for he had perceived the new SPAD unit to have been a 'special squadron' organised to deal with his *Staffel*;

'Our aggressors thought themselves very superior to us because of the excellence of their apparatus. Wolff, my brother and I were flying together. We were three against three. That was as it ought to be.

'Immediately at the beginning of the encounter the aggressive became the defensive. Our superiority became clear. I tackled my opponent and could see how my brother and Wolff each handled their own enemy. The usual waltzing began. We were circling around one another. A favourable wind came to our aid. It drove the fighting away from the Front in the direction of Germany.'

Richthofen got on the tail of Applin, the least experienced of the three;

'I suppose I had smashed up his engine. At any rate, he made up his mind to land. I no longer give pardon to anyone. Therefore, I attacked him a second time and the consequence was that his whole machine fell to pieces. Bits of his aeroplane dropped off like pieces of paper and the body of the machine fell like a stone, burning fiercely. It dropped into a morass. It was impossible to dig it out, and I have never discovered the name of my opponent. He had disappeared. Only the end of the tail was visible, and this marked the place where he had dug his own grave.

'Simultaneously with me, Wolff and my brother had attacked their opponents and had forced them to land not far from my victim.

'We were very happy, and flew home hoping that the anti-Richthofen squadron would often return to the fray.'

Applin, who died near Lecluse, was Richthofen's 49th victory – before the day was over, he would add three more to his score. Harvey-Kelly was shot down at Sailly-en-Ostrevent by Ltn Kurt Wolff and died of head wounds in a German hospital three days later. Hamilton was more fortunate, being forced down at Izel by the Red Baron's younger brother, Ltn Lothar von Richthofen, and taken prisoner.

The loss of Harvey-Kelly was a demoralising blow to No 19 Sqn, and the RFC's 'remedy' was to urge the surviving pilots to fly more missions, which only wore them out. Harvey-Kelly's successor, Maj William D S Sanday, was another 'old hand' from the war's earliest days. He had downed an Albatros two-seater while flying a BE 2c with No 2 Sqn on 11 October 1915, and added three more enemy aeroplanes to his tally flying Sopwith 1½ Strutters with No 70 Sqn. As commander of No 19 Sqn, he continued to pursue an aggressive policy against the Germans, and in May the balance sheet between victories and losses began to improve.

James Child, a North Londoner who had moved to Canada by the time war broke out, sent an Albatros D III down out of control on 25 May for his second victory, concurrently being promoted to captain and getting a Mention in Despatches. He destroyed a DFW C V south-west of Menin on 7 June and later, after a rest from operations, flew SE 5as as a flight leader in the newly-formed No 84 Sqn, bringing his score up to eight on 30 November 1917. Awarded the Military Cross, as well as the Belgian *Croix de Guerre* and Order of Leopold, Child returned to Britain to instruct in February 1918 and then moved back to Canada, where he was killed on 23 August 1918 while trying to rescue an airman from a crash.

Sanday himself achieved acedom when he downed a two-seater near Lille on 13 July. Soon after that, No 19 Sqn was joined by a new Australian replacement pilot by the name of 2Lt Alexander A N D Pentland, who could not have been happier with his posting.

Born in Queensland on 5 August 1894, 'Jerry' Pentland had served in Egypt and at Gallipoli with the 12th Australian Light Horse Regiment, before transferring to the RFC on 21 February 1916. He scored his first victory on 9 June 1916 while with No 16 Sqn, Pentland and his observer, Capt W H Waller, flying a BE 2c. This particular type was considered to be so vulnerable in the air that it was dubbed 'Fokker fodder' by its crews, yet Pentland had succeeded in using the machine to shoot down one of the very *Eindeckers* against which the BE was thought to be 'cold meat'.

Later, while serving as an instructor at London Colney, Pentland made his first acquaintance with the SPAD VII, and he took an instant liking to it. Although he admitted that it had to be flown all the time, and that closing the throttle resulted in a glide angle something akin to that of a brick, he liked the responsiveness of its controls, and its ability to stand up to high-speed dives and the punishment of combat. Even after flying later, more advanced aircraft, Pentland regarded the SPAD VII as the finest fighting machine he ever flew.

Soon after joining No 19 Sqn, the Australian realised that he had to adapt to a more competitive aerial battlefield than he had known in 1916, but he had the benefit of a superb flight leader to teach him the ropes. Like Pentland, Capt Frederick Sowry had scored a previous success in a BE 2c, but Sowry's machine had been modified into a single-seat interceptor for use by No 39 (Home Defence) Sqn, and his victim had been Zeppelin L32, destroyed over Billericay on 24 September 1916, for which he received the Distinguished Service Order. Sowry had since downed an Albatros D III on 17 June and a two-seater on 13 July.

Born in Leytonstone, North London, on 20 October 1893, James Martin Child had moved to Canada by the time war broke out in 1914. Transferring to the RFC from the Manchester Regiment in 1916, he served in No 4 Sqn prior to joining No 19 Sqn in July. Child scored one of the latter unit's earliest SPAD victories on 23 April 1917, and his tally stood at three when he left the unit as a captain. Returning to combat that autumn with newly-organised SE 5a-equipped No 84 Sqn, he had downed five more opponents by 30 November. Posted back to England in February 1918 as an instructor, he was killed at Turnberry on 23 August while trying to rescue a fellow airman from the wreckage of a crashed aeroplane (*via Norman Franks*)

In addition to patrols by flights and squadrons, the RFC sometimes operated in wing strength too. Typically, in the case of Maj Richard G Blomfield's 9th Wing, No 19 Sqn's SPADs would rendezvous with the SE 5as of No 56 Sqn and fly a few thousand feet below them, while Sopwith Pups of No 66 Sqn covered both units from an even higher altitude.

Pentland opened his account with No 19 Sqn by sharing in the destruction of an Albatros two-seater with his flight leader on 20 July, and Sowry became an ace the next day by forcing down an Albatros two-seater and then sending an Albatros D III down out of control north-east of Ypres. Pentland destroyed an Albatros D III on 12 August, but on the 16th he discovered that a fighter pilot did not necessarily need to shoot down enemy aircraft to be appreciated.

Spotting German motor transport moving along the road between Menin and Ypres, he swooped down on a strafing run and drove the lead truck into a ditch at an angle that blocked the rest of the convoy. Pentland then found himself under attack by two German fighters, but turned on them and drove them off.

While looking for more ground targets, he was attacked by the same duo, who put holes in his wings before being driven off again. Next, Pentland shot up some German soldiers on the ground, fought two separate engagements with more enemy scouts and finished the patrol by helping a flight of FE 2d pushers that were beset by two-dozen German fighters. Upon landing, Pentland wrote a brief combat report, discreetly omitting the fact that his SPAD (B1660) was so riddled that it had to be written off – and that his leather flying coat had several bullet holes in it as well.

Maj Sanday added a rider of his own to the report, and subsequently the 5th Brigade's Summary of Work included the following remark;

'The work of the RFC in this battle has been so good that it is impossible to individualise. But the RFC did their job, in all its branches, thoroughly, showing skill, great gallantry and plenty of dash and initiative. Please thank them all. I don't want to be invidious when all did so well, but I would like to thank Pentland (19).'

On 17 August Sowry destroyed an Albatros D III west of Roulers while flying SPAD B3620, which subsequently became Pentland's regular mount. On the 20th Sowry, Pentland and Lt H C Ainger sent an Albatros two-seater down out of control south-east of the Houthulst Forest.

On 26 August, Pentland led Lts Ainger, A R Boeree, R L Graham and J G S Candy on a lightning raid 25 kilometres in German territory to strike at Marcke aerodrome – then the base of Richthofen's *Jasta* 11. On the way, they encountered two DFW C Vs, one of which swerved away, although the second aircraft turned and flew right across the flight's path and then through it, running a gauntlet of gunfire in the process. As it spiralled down, Pentland, the lowest in the flight, gave the DFW a final burst that sent it crashing in a field near Moorseele at 0540 hrs.

Five minutes later the SPADs reached Marcke, where they found eight Albatros fighters on the ground, one of which Pentland noted was all red. Pleased to have caught the Red Baron's Circus napping, the quintet strafed the aeroplanes, and anything else of strategic value, then scattered and headed for home independently. On the way, Pentland strafed a train until his gun jammed, joined Graham in an attack on a German two-seater, during which he got his weapon to fire again, and then engaged an

By the time he arrived at No 19 Sqn in mid-1917, Australian 2Lt A A N D Pentland had already downed a Fokker *Eindecker* while flying a BE 2c with No 16 Sqn on 9 June 1916. Adding a further nine victories flying SPADs, Capt 'Jerry' Pentland is seen here beside a Sopwith Dolphin of No 87 Sqn, with which he scored an additional 13 victories in 1918 (*via Norman Franks*)

Seated in a BE 2c of No 39 (Home Defence) Sqn, 2Lt Frederick Sowry opened his account by destroying Zeppelin L32 on 24 September 1916. He went on to lead a flight within No 19 Sqn, adding 12 aeroplanes to his score between 17 June and 15 October 1917 (*via Norman Franks*)

Albatros scout that was attacking him until it disengaged. At that point, Pentland concluded in his report, 'I came home for all I was worth!' All five pilots were credited with the DFW, and Pentland was subsequently awarded the MC for his role in the Marcke raid.

Richthofen's reaction was mixed. He was chagrined at seeing three of his Albatros D Vs put out of commission. On the other hand, on 18 August, he had received an order from Generalleutnant Ernst von Hoeppner, commander of the *Luftstreitskräfte*, stating that he 'fly only when absolute necessity justifies it', and the SPAD attack duly gave him such a justification. He took off, accompanied by his four remaining fighters, in pursuit of the raiders.

Posted to No 19 Sqn in November 1917, Canadian-born Capt Arthur Bradfield Fairclough scored nine victories in SPADs between 6 and 29 December, and another five flying Sopwith Dolphins between 17 March and 2 May 1918. Later transferring to Dolphin-equipped No 23 Sqn, he had increased his total to 19 by 5 July. Fairclough was awarded the Military Cross in March 1918 (*via Norman Franks*)

He failed to catch them, but he did run into another lone SPAD of No 19 Sqn, flown by 2Lt Collingsby P Williams, who he chased into a cloud. Moments later, Williams' aeroplane exploded in mid-air, but faulty incendiary ammunition set fire to Richthofen's pressure line and engine as well, and he was fortunate to glide his damaged machine to safety. The Red Baron's 59th victim was also his last to be scored in an Albatros D V before changing over to the Fokker Dr I triplane, and the last casualty that he would inflict on No 19 Sqn.

Pentland finished August with an Albatros D V out of control on the 31st. On 11 September Sowry and Ainger downed a Rumpler east of Quesnoy, while Pentland destroyed another south of Bousbecque. The Australian downed yet another Rumpler on 15 September, followed by an Albatros D V the next day and an 'enemy scout' on the 23rd. Sowry sent a D V down out of control on the 20th, and on the 30th he shared in driving an Albatros two-seater down out of control with Lts Delamere, R M Strang, R A Hewat, J G S Candy and an SE 5a from another unit.

SPAD B.6776 shows yet another variation in No 19 Sqn's unit markings – two red or black bands and the letter 'B' on the fuselage side. Lt Eric Olivier sent a German two-seater down out of control south-west of Gheluwe in this machine on 26 October 1917, but the following day the fighter was brought down north of Wervicq by Ltn Karl Adolf Seifert of *Jasta* 24s. The SPAD's pilot, 2Lt L Whitehouse, was duly taken prisoner. Flying SPAD VII A.6714, Olivier had scored five more victories by 22 December. Transitioning to the Dolphin early in the new year, he had increased his tally to eight come 17 March 1918 (*via Leslie Rogers*)

On 26 September, Pentland was injured when his SPAD was struck by an artillery shell. Awarded the MC, he initially served as an instructor after his recovery, before being posted to No 87 Sqn as a flight commander. Applying the 'lone wolf' tactics he had employed in SPADs to Sopwith Dolphins, he had raised his score to 23 by 25 August 1918, when he was wounded in the foot in a fight with *Jasta* 57. This injury spelled the end of World War 1 for Pentland, but hardly the end of his flying career.

He flew in the post-war Royal Australian Air Force (RAAF) and in the gold fields of New Guinea, before becoming a pilot for Australian National Airways in 1930. During World War 2, Pentland ran an air-sea rescue service in the Pacific, and retired from the RAAF with the rank of squadron leader and the Australian Flying Cross. By the time of his death at Bayview, in New South Wales in 1983, 'Jerry' Pentland had lived one of the more swashbuckling sagas of the early air age.

Another SPAD ace who distinguished himself in the autumn of 1917 was Capt John Leacroft, who had served as an observer in No 14 Sqn in Egypt early on in the war, before training as a pilot and joining No 19 Sqn. His first victory came on 17 June, followed by successes over Albatros D Vs on 6 July and 26 August. In September, however, he truly came into his stride, downing two D Vs on the 1st, another on the 3rd, two more on the 19th, one on the 21st and a two-seater on the 25th. Leacroft added more Albatros D Vs to his account on 12 and 21 October, and sent two more down out of control on the 24th, taking his score to 14. He was then withdrawn for a rest, but returned to No 19 Sqn in early 1918.

Now flying Dolphins, Leacroft survived being shot down twice and increased his total to 22 kills. He served on in the post-war RAF until 1937, rejoining the service during World War 2. Retiring again to Bexhill with the rank of group captain, John Leacroft died in 1971.

October 1917 saw Fred Sowry claim a Fokker D V destroyed on the 7th, an Albatros two-seater shared with Hewat and Candy on the 9th, and another Albatros two-seater destroyed in flames north-east of Moorseele on the 15th. After that, Sowry received the MC and was posted back to England to spend the rest of the war as CO of No 143 (Home Defence) Sqn. Continuing his service in the RAF until 1940, Fred Sowry retired as a group captain and settled in Eastbourne, Sussex, where he died in 1969. His son, Frederick B Sowry, also made a career of the RAF, becoming an air vice-marshal and later president of *Cross & Cockade* International, an organisation dedicated to the study of World War I aviation history.

While No 19 Sqn was receiving its SPADs, a second unit on the Western Front – No 23 Sqn – began exchanging its FE 2bs and Martinsyde G 100 Elephants for SPAD VIIs in February 1917. By June, the unit was engaged over Flanders in the Third Battle of Ypres, and like No 19 Sqn, trading blows with some of the best fighter units in the *Luftstreitkräfte*.

Indisputably the highest-scoring SPAD ace in the RFC was No 23 Sqn's William John Charles Kennedy Cochran-Patrick. Born in Ireland on 25 May 1896 and educated at Cambridge University, he had served in the Rifle Brigade before joining the RFC. After qualifying as a pilot in April 1915, Lt Cochran-Patrick proved to be such a skilful flyer that he was assigned the job of a test pilot at No 1 Aeroplane Depot at St Omer. There, he probably would have stayed, had a German two-seater not chanced to stage a long-range flight over his area on 26 April 1916.

A professional soldier from Pointe de Butte, New Brunswick, in Canada, Maj Albert Desbrisay Carter scored his first two SPAD victories with No 19 Sqn on 31 October, and had raised his total to 15 by 29 December. He resumed his scoring in Dolphins with another 'double' on 15 March 1918, and had increased his tally to 29 by 16 May. Three days later, however, Carter was brought down by Ltn Paul Billik of *Jasta* 52. Repatriated to Britain on 13 December 1918, Carter was killed on 22 May 1919 when the Fokker D VII he was test-flying broke up in flight (*via Norman Franks*)

Taking off in Nieuport 5172, Cochran-Patrick attacked the intruder three times until it crashed near Hazebrouck, then landed alongside it only to find the crew, Unteroffizier Hans Hviires and Ltn Georg Jesko von Puttkammer of *Kampfgeschwader* 5, dead. That action earned Cochran-Patrick an MC, and a transfer to No 70 Sqn, equipped with Sopwith 1^1/$_2$ Strutters, in which he scored two more victories on 14 and 15 September 1916 – on both occasions his observers, 2Lt E W Burke and Capt F G Glenday, were killed in the course of the actions.

Promoted to captain, Cochran-Patrick was reassigned to No 23 Sqn in 1917, where he reopened his account – and became an ace – by driving two Albatros D IIIs down out of control on 22 April. He was credited with a two-seater out of control on 26 April, and ended the month with an Albatros D III in flames over Inchy-en-Barrois, his victim possibly being Ltn Friedrich Mallinkrodt (a six-victory ace of *Jasta* 20) who was wounded. Cochran-Patrick downed a D III out of control on 2 May, and was flying SPAD B1580, which would figure in all of his subsequent successes, when he downed yet another Albatros D III in flames west of Bourlon Wood on the 11th. This time the pilot, 11-victory ace Offizier-stellvertreter Edmund Nathanael of *Jasta* 5, was killed.

Cochran-Patrick shared in bringing down two D IIIs on 13 May and destroyed another exactly one week later. Four more enemy aeroplanes fell to his guns in June, and he scored two more 'doubles' on 6 and 7 July. On 16 July, he destroyed an Albatros D V for his 21st, and final, victory, at which point he was promoted to major and given command of No 60 Sqn. He had also been awarded a bar to his MC and later the DSO.

At the end of 1917, Cochran-Patrick returned to England to serve in the Training Division of the Air Board, then came around full circle to No 1 Aeroplane Depot in 1918. After the war, he did a lot of aerial survey work, but was killed in an air crash in Johannesburg, South Africa, on 27 September 1933.

On 27 July 1917 Ltn Heinrich Kroll (the German ace who had killed René Dorme two months earlier, and who had since taken command of *Jasta* 24s) got an object lesson on the folly of underestimating SPADs;

'I attacked ten SPADs and brought one out of the formation. Using every possible manoeuvre, I circled with him from 4000 metres down to

A graduate of the Royal Military College at Sandhurst, Major Patrick Huskinson joined the RFC in 1915 and earned the MC whilst serving with No 2 Sqn. Posted to No 19 Sqn in 1917, he had scored seven kills in SPAD VIIs by 6 January 1918 – four of them in B.1593 – and another four flying Dolphin C.3792. In spite of being blinded in an air raid during World War 2, he designed the 4000-lb 'block-buster' bomb, and retired from the RAF with the rank of air commodore (*via Norman Franks*)

Delivered to No 23 Sqn on 8 June 1917, B'3504 was lost just 11 days later when it was downed by a two-seater of *Flieger Abteilung* 33, and its pilot, Capt T Davidson, made a PoW. Powered by a 180-hp Hispano-Suiza 8Ab engine, this aircraft had had its radiator cowling painted in blue and red segments (*via Leslie Rogers*)

Irish-born Capt William John Charles Kennedy Cochran-Patrick was flying a Nieuport on 26 April 1916 when he scored his first victory – an LVG C I – while serving as a test pilot at No 1 Aeroplane Depot at St Omer. He later received the Military Cross for this action. Posted to a frontline unit, Cochran-Patrick scored two victories in Sopwith 1¹/₂ Strutters with No 70 Sqn, before joining No 23 Sqn. Here, he claimed at least 10 of his total of 21 victories in SPAD VII B.1580 between 11 May and 16 July 1917. Post-war Cochran-Patrick undertook aerial survey work, and he was killed in a crash in Johannesburg, South Africa, on 27 September 1933 (*via Norman Franks*)

SPAD VII B'1524 of No 23 Sqn sits forlornly in a German hangar after being brought down near Menin on 7 June 1917 by Offizierstellvertreter Paul Aue of *Jasta* 10 – its wounded pilot, 2Lt F W Illingworth, was taken prisoner. Prior to that day, B'1524 had been used by Capt W J C K Cochran-Patrick to send two Albatros D IIIs down out of control on 22 April 1917, followed by a two-seater four days later (*via Leslie Rogers*)

2500 metres. Then he suddenly turned and went on the offensive. He shot my inlet pipes and induction valves, causing a fire in the carburettor. This is the worst thing that can happen in an air fight since there is a sheet of flames and the pilot is burned alive. However, when this happens, one must not lose his nerve.

'I immediately turned off the petrol, switched off the ignition, and dived steeply! The machine smoked and burned, and my face was full of fuel and oil so that I could not see out of my goggles – I tore them off at 800 metres and looked for a place to land. With a stationary propeller, I pulled up over a row of trees, under a high tension cable, took some telephone wires with me, and landed in an open field where the machine came to rest on its nose. I was not in the least hurt, and was able to thank God that I had had such a deliverance! But my poor machine – my grey and white steed – was completely broken.'

Kroll, who at least survived his encounter, had been the victim of a SPAD VII of No 23 Sqn, but his adversary had been American – one of many who had quietly entered the RFC while their more flamboyant *Lafayette* colleagues were attracting all the attention in French service. Born in Norfolk, Virginia, on 30 June 1892, Clive Wilson Warman abandoned a civil engineering practice to join the Canadian infantry in August 1914 and, after being wounded in May 1915, transferring to the RFC.

Posted to No 23 Sqn in May 1917, he opened his account with an Albatros D III over Thorout on 6 July, his opponent possibly being Vfw Fritz Loerzer of *Jasta* 26, who was slightly wounded. After destroying a two-seater on 13 July, Capt Warman was credited with an Albatros 'out of control' north of Menin on 27 July – Kroll's Albatros D V 2075/17 represented his third victory in a fortnight. Warman finished the month with an Albatros D III destroyed on the 31st, and became on ace when he burned a balloon on 9 August.

Usually alternating between SPAD B1698 and B1581, Warman downed two Albatros D Vs on 12 August (one of which was shared with Lt Standish Conn O'Grady, an Irish member of No 23 Sqn who would survive the war with nine victories). Two more were destroyed three days later, and a DFW C V and a balloon claimed on the 16th.

Following the latter combat, Warman had to fight his way through three German fighters, during which his machine gun jammed and he ended up firing his Very light at them. Finally, out of a combination of desperation and frustration, he threw the small hammer used for clearing gun jams at the nearest fighter, before finally returning to his aerodrome in disgust.

After adding another Albatros D V to his score on 18 August, Warman was awarded the DSO and MC, and made a flight leader, but on 20 August he was grievously wounded and spent nearly a year recovering. Assigned in February 1919 to No 1 Canadian Sqn, Royal Canadian Air Force, Clive Warman crashed into a sewage farm and subsequently died in hospital in Edmonton, British Columbia, on 12 June 1919.

At the end of 1917 SPAD XIIIs began to replace the SPAD VIIs, particularly in No 23 Sqn, but between February and March 1918, both this unit and No 19 Sqn were re-equipped with an indigenously built fighter whose airframe, like the SPADs, was based on the Hispano-Suiza engine, – the Sopwith Dolphin.

The SPAD VII had served the RFC for little more than a year, and only two units were fully equipped with it, but they made a sizeable impression. Eleven of No 19 Sqn's aces scored at least one of their victories while flying SPADs, as did 16 of No 23 Sqn's leading lights. The dismissive remarks that Manfred von Richthofen had made in April 1917 regarding the SPADs of the 'Anti-Richthofen Squadron' proved to be more than a little premature.

A VARIETY OF MARKINGS

For a mere two squadrons on the Western Front (along with additional aircraft parcelled out to units in the Middle East and Salonika), RFC SPAD VIIs came in a remarkable variety of colours and liveries. French-supplied SPADs were delivered in the usual clear-doped fabric with buff-painted cowlings, but some British-built examples were delivered with natural metal cowls and light grey fabric, or with part or all of the uppersurfaces finished in P.C.10 green or P.C.12 brown camouflage.

The earliest SPAD VIIs in No 19 Sqn were marked with a black dumbbell on the fuselage, as had been previously worn by the unit's BE 12s. In May, however, that marking was largely replaced by red, white and blue stripes around the fuselage and roundels on the wheel discs, which had been applied after a SPAD had been fired on in error by a British aircraft.

The dumb-bell insignia was revived around 16 August 1917, appearing in white on camouflaged aircraft. Later in the month, the idea of using a white square aft of the fuselage roundel was discussed, although it does not seem to have been adopted. By October, the dumb-bell had been replaced again, this time by various coloured fuselage bands and letters – apparently A, B or C to denote the flight. This state of affairs prevailed until January 1918, when the first Dolphins arrived to replace the SPADs, and a white dumb-bell was applied to the fuselage sides once more – where it remained for the duration of the war.

There does not seem to have been any serious attempt to standardise a marking system for No 23 Sqn until 26 August 1917, when a triangle appeared aft of the fuselage roundels, and an individual letter aft of that. At various times prior to that date, some of the unit's aircraft had stripes on the cowlings and bands and numerals on the fuselage, these coming and going on the basis of various flights' policies.

One of the leading SPAD VII exponents within No 23 Sqn was Capt Clive Wilson Warman, an American who joined the Canadian infantry and then transferred to the RFC in 1917. He was credited with ten enemy aeroplanes and two balloons up to 18 August 1917, but was then wounded two days later. Awarded the DSO and MC, Warman was killed in a flying accident with No 1 Canadian Sqn on 12 June 1919 (*via Norman Franks*)

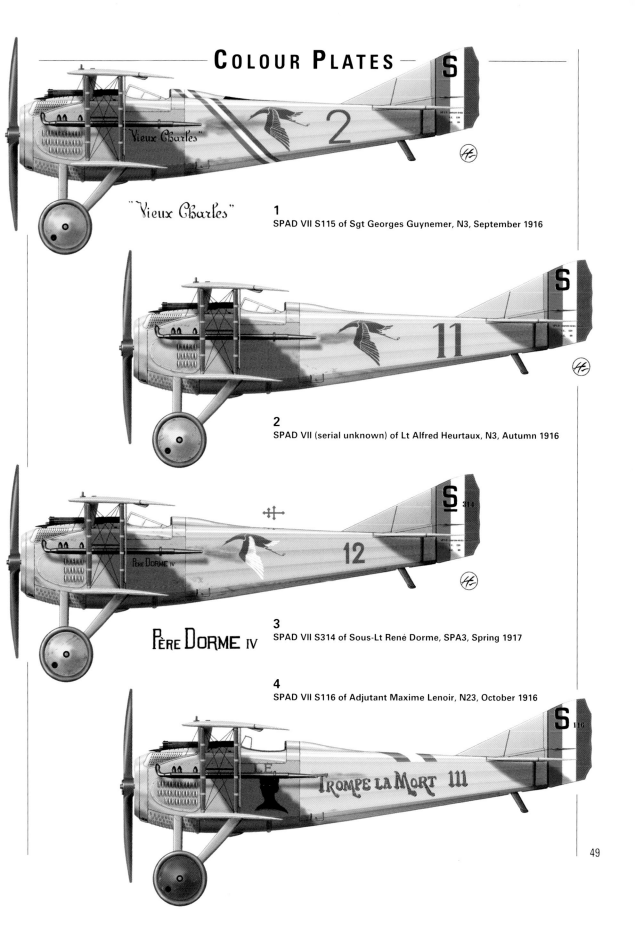

"Vieux Charles"

1
SPAD VII S115 of Sgt Georges Guynemer, N3, September 1916

2
SPAD VII (serial unknown) of Lt Alfred Heurtaux, N3, Autumn 1916

PÈRE DORME IV

3
SPAD VII S314 of Sous-Lt René Dorme, SPA3, Spring 1917

4
SPAD VII S116 of Adjutant Maxime Lenoir, N23, October 1916

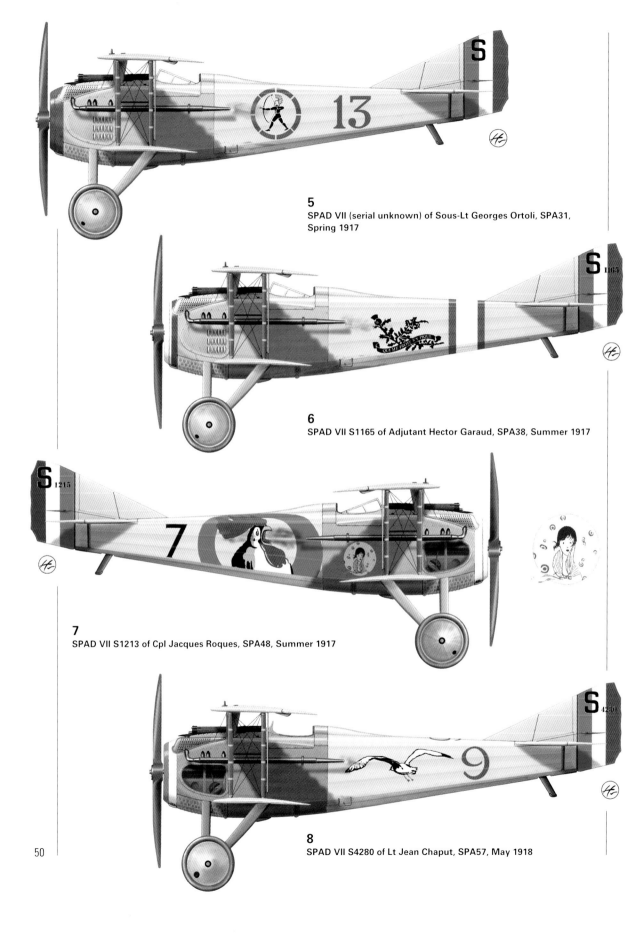

5
SPAD VII (serial unknown) of Sous-Lt Georges Ortoli, SPA31,
Spring 1917

6
SPAD VII S1165 of Adjutant Hector Garaud, SPA38, Summer 1917

7
SPAD VII S1213 of Cpl Jacques Roques, SPA48, Summer 1917

8
SPAD VII S4280 of Lt Jean Chaput, SPA57, May 1918

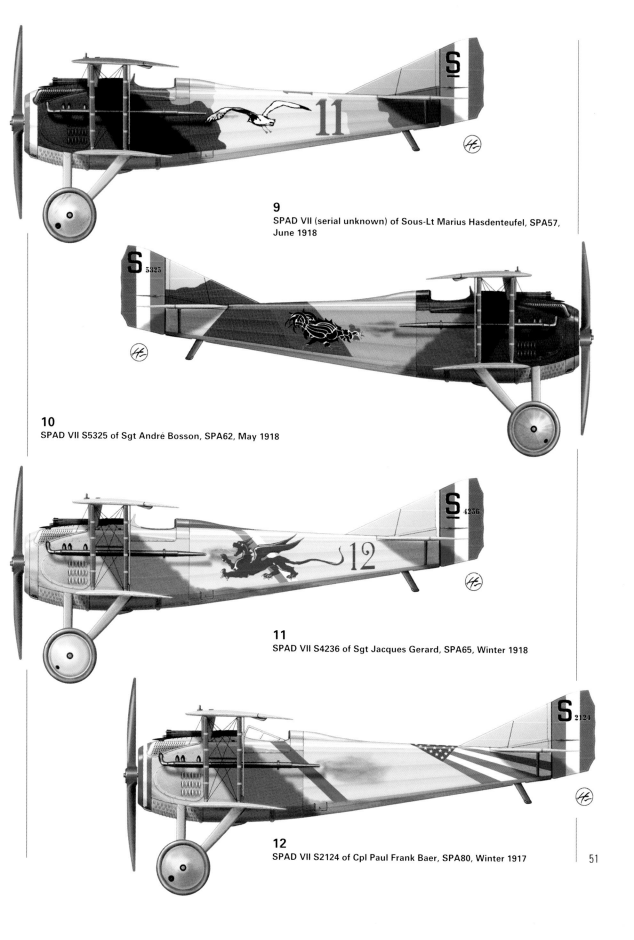

9
SPAD VII (serial unknown) of Sous-Lt Marius Hasdenteufel, SPA57,
June 1918

10
SPAD VII S5325 of Sgt André Bosson, SPA62, May 1918

11
SPAD VII S4236 of Sgt Jacques Gerard, SPA65, Winter 1918

12
SPAD VII S2124 of Cpl Paul Frank Baer, SPA80, Winter 1917

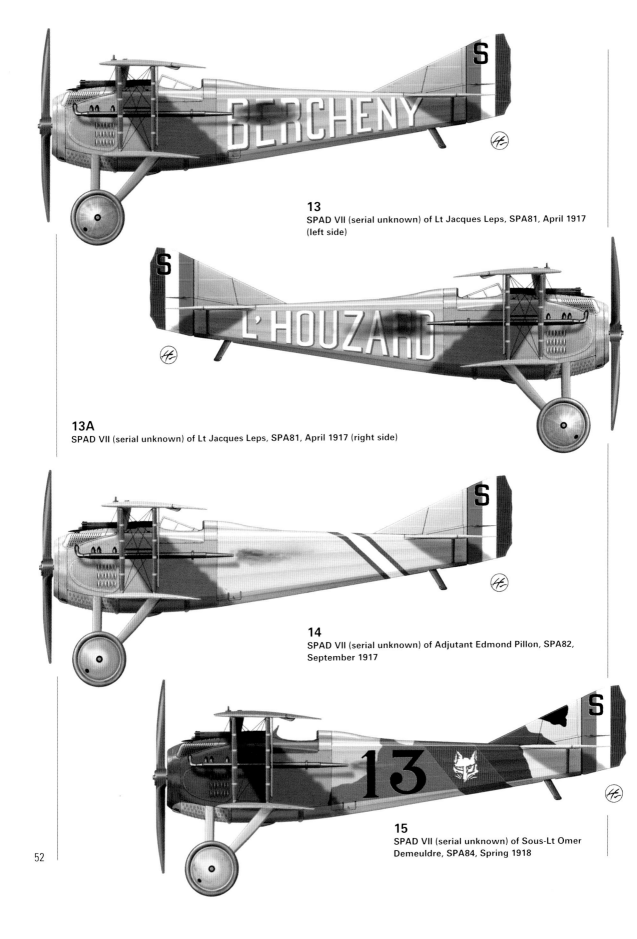

13
SPAD VII (serial unknown) of Lt Jacques Leps, SPA81, April 1917
(left side)

13A
SPAD VII (serial unknown) of Lt Jacques Leps, SPA81, April 1917 (right side)

14
SPAD VII (serial unknown) of Adjutant Edmond Pillon, SPA82,
September 1917

15
SPAD VII (serial unknown) of Sous-Lt Omer
Demeuldre, SPA84, Spring 1918

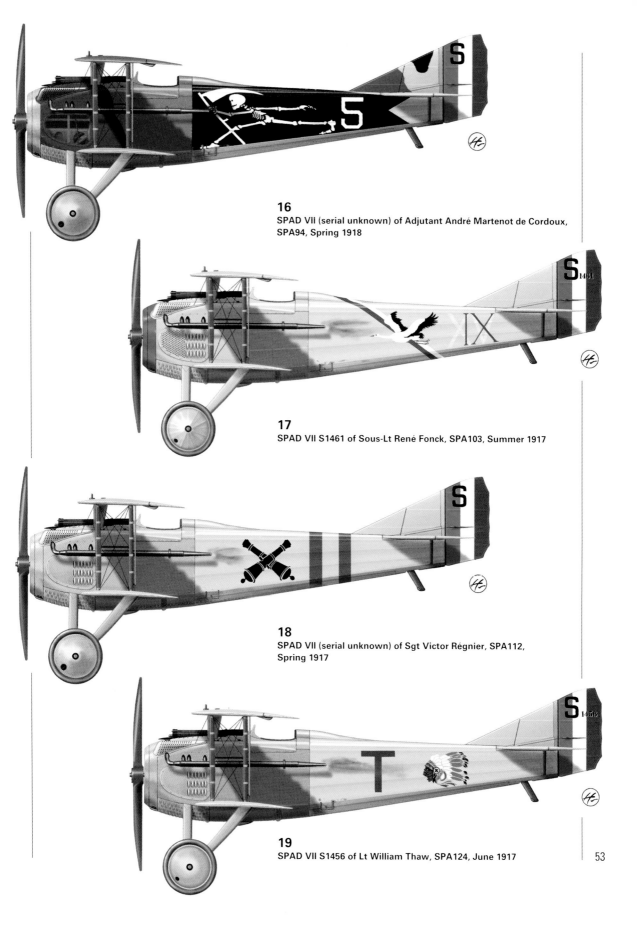

16
SPAD VII (serial unknown) of Adjutant André Martenot de Cordoux,
SPA94, Spring 1918

17
SPAD VII S1461 of Sous-Lt René Fonck, SPA103, Summer 1917

18
SPAD VII (serial unknown) of Sgt Victor Régnier, SPA112,
Spring 1917

19
SPAD VII S1456 of Lt William Thaw, SPA124, June 1917

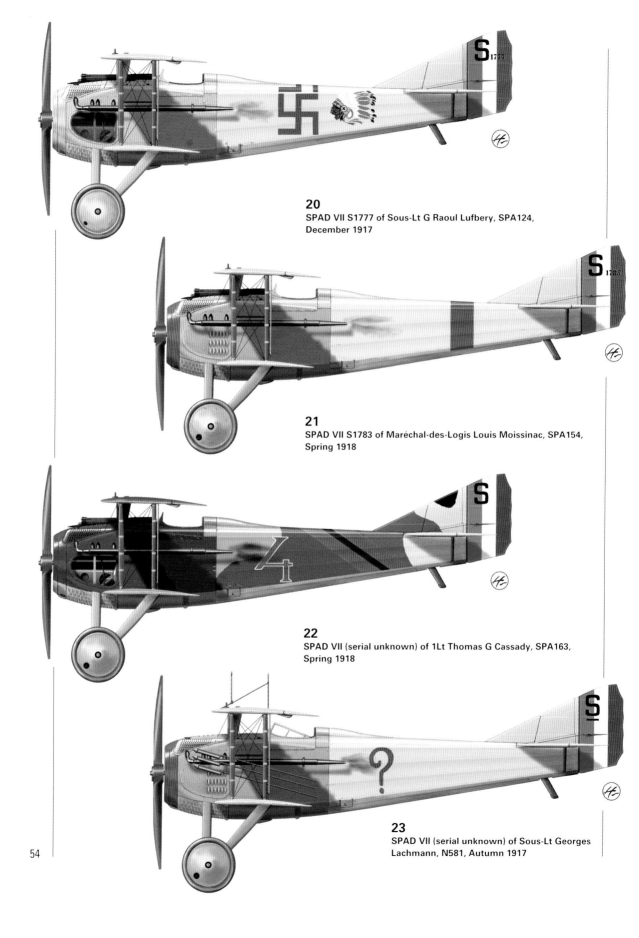

20
SPAD VII S1777 of Sous-Lt G Raoul Lufbery, SPA124,
December 1917

21
SPAD VII S1783 of Maréchal-des-Logis Louis Moissinac, SPA154,
Spring 1918

22
SPAD VII (serial unknown) of 1Lt Thomas G Cassady, SPA163,
Spring 1918

23
SPAD VII (serial unknown) of Sous-Lt Georges
Lachmann, N581, Autumn 1917

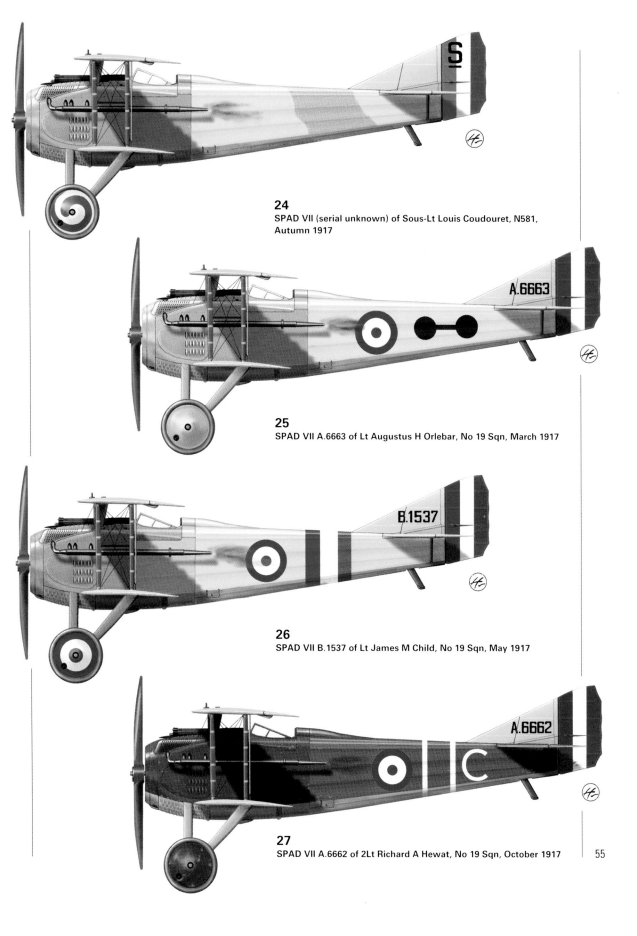

24
SPAD VII (serial unknown) of Sous-Lt Louis Coudouret, N581,
Autumn 1917

25
SPAD VII A.6663 of Lt Augustus H Orlebar, No 19 Sqn, March 1917

26
SPAD VII B.1537 of Lt James M Child, No 19 Sqn, May 1917

27
SPAD VII A.6662 of 2Lt Richard A Hewat, No 19 Sqn, October 1917

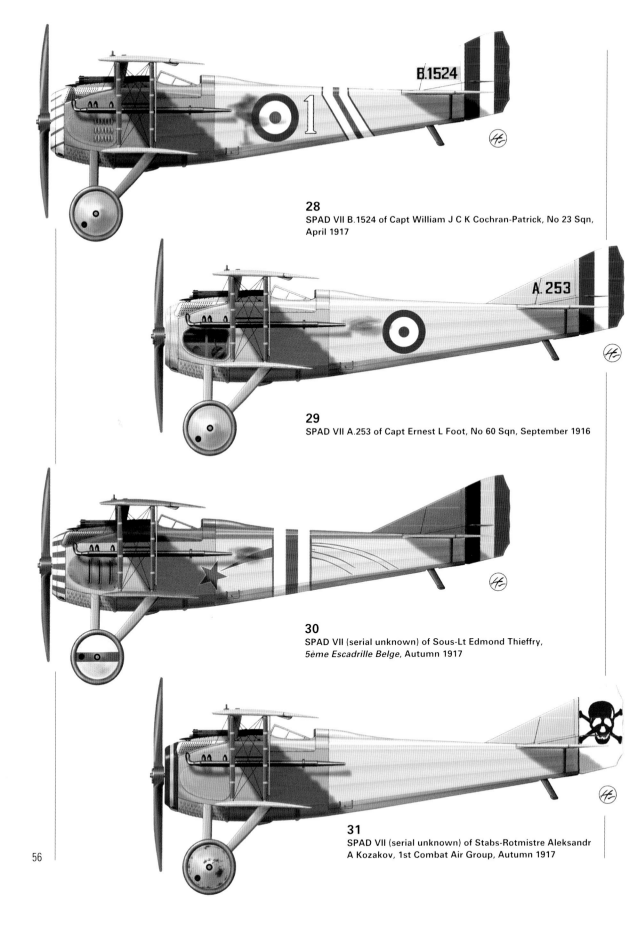

28
SPAD VII B.1524 of Capt William J C K Cochran-Patrick, No 23 Sqn,
April 1917

29
SPAD VII A.253 of Capt Ernest L Foot, No 60 Sqn, September 1916

30
SPAD VII (serial unknown) of Sous-Lt Edmond Thieffry,
5ème Escadrille Belge, Autumn 1917

31
SPAD VII (serial unknown) of Stabs-Rotmistre Aleksandr
A Kozakov, 1st Combat Air Group, Autumn 1917

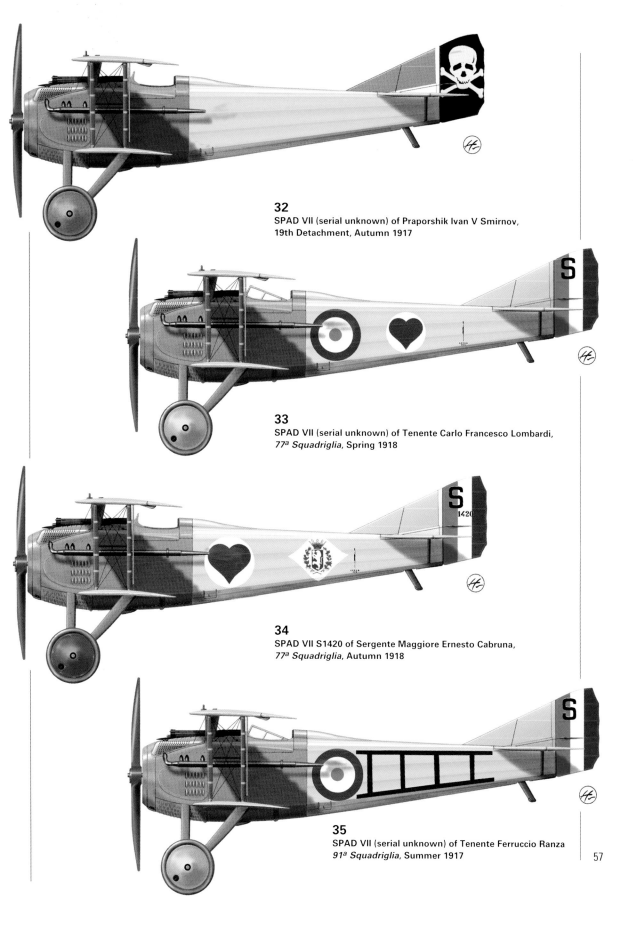

32
SPAD VII (serial unknown) of Praporshik Ivan V Smirnov,
19th Detachment, Autumn 1917

33
SPAD VII (serial unknown) of Tenente Carlo Francesco Lombardi,
77ª Squadriglia, Spring 1918

34
SPAD VII S1420 of Sergente Maggiore Ernesto Cabruna,
77ª Squadriglia, Autumn 1918

35
SPAD VII (serial unknown) of Tenente Ferruccio Ranza
91ª Squadriglia, Summer 1917

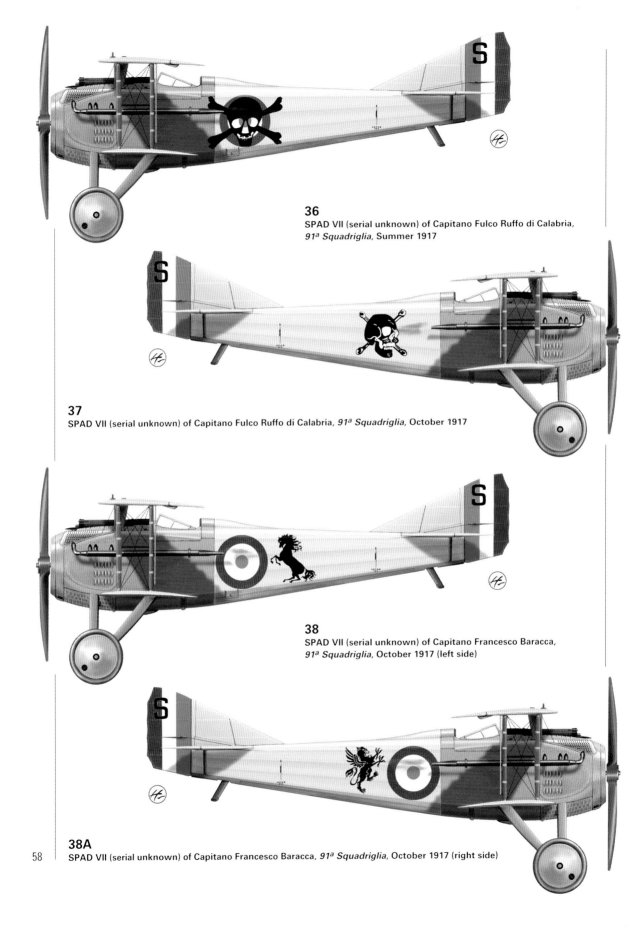

36
SPAD VII (serial unknown) of Capitano Fulco Ruffo di Calabria,
91ª Squadriglia, Summer 1917

37
SPAD VII (serial unknown) of Capitano Fulco Ruffo di Calabria, *91ª Squadriglia*, October 1917

38
SPAD VII (serial unknown) of Capitano Francesco Baracca,
91ª Squadriglia, October 1917 (left side)

38A
SPAD VII (serial unknown) of Capitano Francesco Baracca, *91ª Squadriglia*, October 1917 (right side)

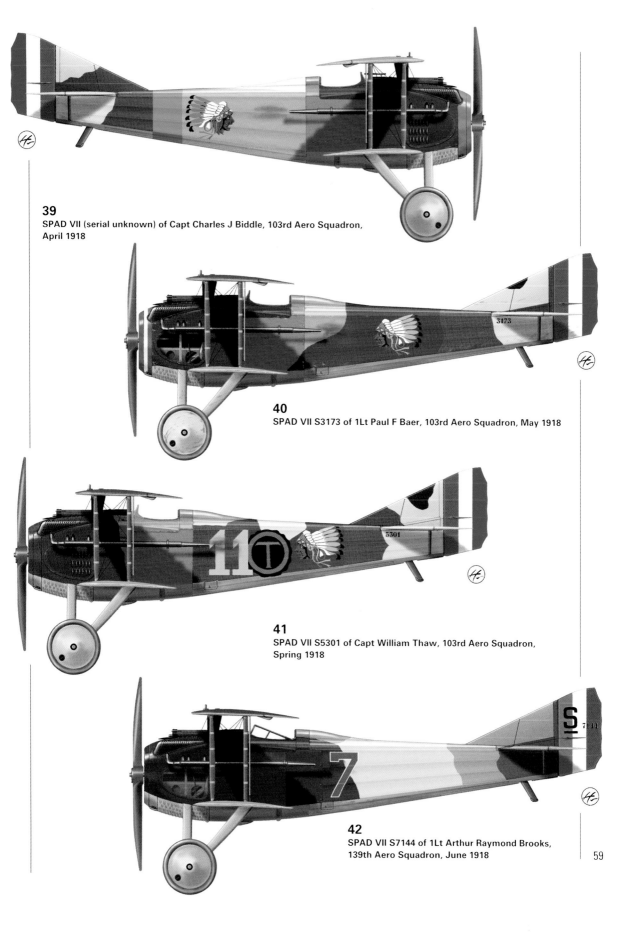

39
SPAD VII (serial unknown) of Capt Charles J Biddle, 103rd Aero Squadron,
April 1918

40
SPAD VII S3173 of 1Lt Paul F Baer, 103rd Aero Squadron, May 1918

41
SPAD VII S5301 of Capt William Thaw, 103rd Aero Squadron,
Spring 1918

42
SPAD VII S7144 of 1Lt Arthur Raymond Brooks,
139th Aero Squadron, June 1918

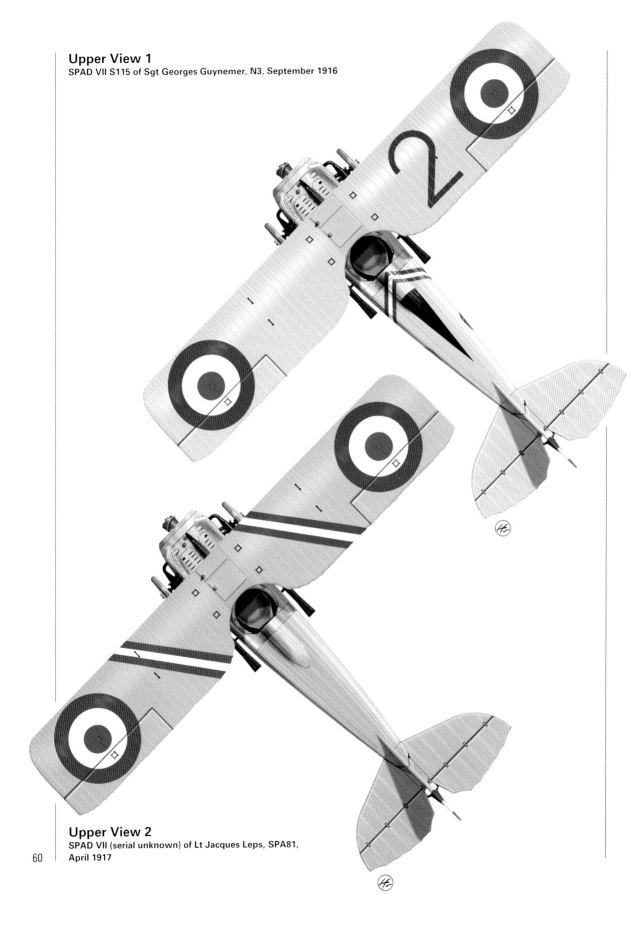

Upper View 1
SPAD VII S115 of Sgt Georges Guynemer, N3, September 1916

Upper View 2
SPAD VII (serial unknown) of Lt Jacques Leps, SPA81,
April 1917

Upper View 3
SPAD VII (serial unknown) of Adjutant Edmond Pillon, SPA82, September 1917

Upper View 4
SPAD VII (serial unknown) of Sous-Lt Omer Demeuldre,
SPA84, Spring 1918

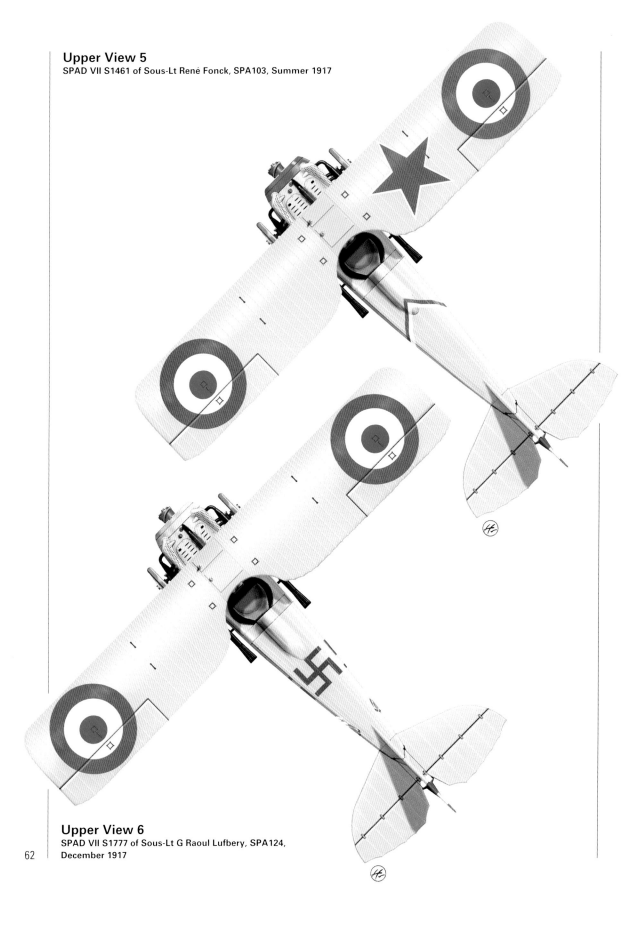

Upper View 5
SPAD VII S1461 of Sous-Lt René Fonck, SPA103, Summer 1917

Upper View 6
SPAD VII S1777 of Sous-Lt G Raoul Lufbery, SPA124,
December 1917

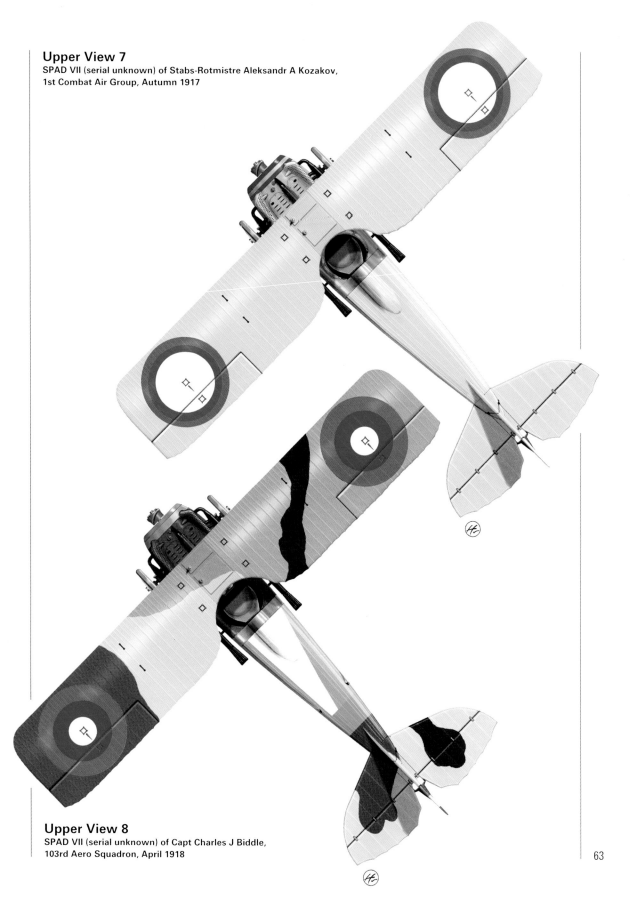

Upper View 7
SPAD VII (serial unknown) of Stabs-Rotmistre Aleksandr A Kozakov,
1st Combat Air Group, Autumn 1917

Upper View 8
SPAD VII (serial unknown) of Capt Charles J Biddle,
103rd Aero Squadron, April 1918

SPAD VIIs FOR THE ALLIES

Belgian Ace

Although driven from their own country in 1914, the men of the Belgian Air Service fought on, mainly with French equipment. And of the five aces Belgium produced, only one flew a single-seat SPAD – Edmond Thieffry.

Born in Etterbeek, near Brussels, on 28 September 1892, Thieffry was studying law at Louvain University when he was conscripted into the army in 1912, serving in the *14e Régiment de Ligne* until January 1914. He then resumed his studies, completing them just days before war broke out. Serving in the *10e Régiment de Ligne*, he was captured by the Germans but escaped on an old motorbike to the Netherlands, where he was interned, but eventually obtained a release. Soon after rejoining his old unit on the Yser front, Thieffry decided to transfer to aviation, and earned his military brevet at Etampes on 21 September 1915. He was at first assigned to fly Voisin and Farman reconnaissance aircraft in the *4e Escadrille*, and after some 80 combat missions, his aggressive nature led his commander to recommend that he change to single-seaters.

On 11 December 1916, Thieffry joined the *5e Escadrille*, equipped with Nieuport 11s. He soon demonstrated his fearlessness by flying over German-occupied Brussels on 24 January 1917 and dropping leaflets to his family, his fiancée and on his old school. On the evening of 15 March, he shot down a German two-seater, followed by another eight days later.

Thieffry's score had risen to four by the early summer of 1917, when his unit was re-equipped with Nieuport 17s. On 3 July he downed two Albatros D IIIs north of Dixmude for his fifth and sixth victories, this being the first 'double haul' credited to a Belgian fighter pilot. As a reward for his efforts, Thieffry was commissioned a sous-lieutenant, made a *Chevalier de l'Ordre de Léopold*, awarded the *Croix de Guerre Belge* and personally decorated by King Vittorio Emmanuele of Italy in September.

On 15 August, the first of an eventual 15 SPAD VIIs to be delivered to the *Aviation Militaire Belge* arrived – purchased by an upper-class Belgian prince, they were presented as a gift to the *5e Escadrille*. Given the serial number Sp 1, it was assigned to Thieffry, who flew his first combat sortie in it the very next day – and shot down an Albatros two-seater over the Houthulst Forest for his seventh victory.

Thieffry's next victim (on 22 August) was a fighter of Marine *Feldjagdstaffel I*, Flugzeug Ober Maat Luitjen Luitjens being killed.

Sous-Lt Edmond Thieffry is seen sitting in SPAD VII Sp 1 soon after it was delivered to the Belgian air service in July 1917. Later applying both the comet insignia of the *5ème Escadrille Belge* and his personal markings to the fighter, Thieffry scored his seventh through ninth kills in it on 16, 22 and 26 August, respectively, but was in turn shot down in it on 31 August (*Centre for Historical Documentation, BAF*)

Thieffry emerges from the cockpit of Sp 1, dressed in the protective garb necessary for high-altitude flying in an open cockpit, even in summertime (*Aviation Society of Antwerp vzw, via Walter Pieters*)

Thieffry downed another enemy fighter over Slype four days later, although on this occasion the pilot, Uffz Karl Conradt of *Jasta* 17, survived the engagement. However, on 31 August, during one of his lone patrols, Thieffry encountered two Albatros D Vs west of Dixmude and found himself outmatched. Ltn Karl Hammes of *Jasta* 35b stuck to the SPAD's tail until his bullets set the fuel tank alight. Thieffry escaped death by means of an unusual feature incorporated into all SPADs – the ability to jettison the fuel tank. He duly crash-landed behind the Belgian trench line.

Obtaining a new SPAD, which he decorated in his red and white livery, Thieffry resumed hunting, and on 16 October he brought down another enemy scout at Merckem. He then claimed a two-seater over Oostkerke on 9 November, although this could not be confirmed – the last of five 'probables' in addition to his ten confirmed victories.

Thieffry's luck finally ran out on 23 February 1918. Patrolling in company with adjutants André de Meulemeester and Georges Baron Kervijn de Lettenhove of the *1ème Escadrille*, he attacked a German two-seater piloted by Gefreiter Lunecke of *Flieger Abteilung* 227 over Clercken, but he waited a moment too long to open fire and the German observer, Ltn Sanbold, hit the ace's SPAD first with a fatal shot. Last seen by de Meulemeester and de Lettenhove spinning down over Woumen with his fuel tank on fire, Thieffry was given up for dead by his comrades for several weeks, until they learned that he was, in fact, wounded and a prisoner.

Thieffry escaped on 13 April, but was recaptured in the Black Forest ten days later. Held at Bad Aibling, Ingolstadt, Fort Orft, Fort X and Fort 8, he did not return to Brussels until 6 December 1918.

Although he became a lawyer and politician after the war, Thieffry never lost his taste for flying, and on 12 February 1925, he and Léopold Roger set out to make the first flight to Léopoldville, in the Belgian Congo – an odyssey that took them 51 days. Thieffry continued working to establish an airline to the colony until 29 April 1929, when his Avimeta CM 92 was caught in a tropical storm and crashed 150 miles from Alberville, killing Thieffry and Gaston Julien, although their mechanic, Eugéne Gastuche, survived. Edmund Thieffry was posthumously made an *Officier de l'Ordre Léopold I* for his work in the Congo.

Italian Aces

Although Italy produced competent reconnaissance and float aircraft, and its Caproni multi-engine bombers were among the best of their kind in the world in 1915, it never managed to develop a successful indigenous fighter during World War 1. Instead, its air force initially had to rely on licence-built French Nieuport 11s and 17s and Hanriot HD 1s.

In March 1917, *77ª Squadriglia da Caccia* received its first SPAD VIIs, and this type gradually supplanted its Nieuport 17s. Other Italian units received SPADs as complements to their normal Nieuport or Hanriot equipment as well, but the only other squadron to be completely equipped with the type was *91ª Squadriglia*.

Although overshadowed by the more famous *91ª*, *77ª Squadriglia* produced its share of SPAD heroes too, such as Carlo Francesco Lombardi and Ernesto Cabruna.

Born in Genoa on 21 January 1897, 'Francis' Lombardi, as he was universally known, served in the infantry, before training as a reserve

SPAD VII Sᴘ 2, flown by Sous-Lt Charles Ciselet of the *5ème Escadrille Belge*, shows that unit's red and white comet emblem, as well as the bands and stripes that pilots often used for individual identification. The unit's sole ace, Sous-Lt Edmond Thieffry, marked his SPAD (Sᴘ 1) in a similar style

Thieffry poses with his second SPAD VII, which bore a more flamboyant variation on his red and white band markings, and in which he scored his 10th, and final, victory on 16 October 1917 (*Aviation Society of Antwerp vzw, via Walter Pieters*)

officer and earning his flying certificate in Blériots at the Venaria Reale School on 16 May 1916. After serving as an instructor, he finally got a fighting assignment to *77ª Squadriglia* on 23 August 1917.

Flying Nieuport 17s during and after the Battle of Caporetto, he scored his first kill on 26 October when he forced Lohner flying boat K212 to crash into Lake Doberdó. The following day Lombardi claimed two more aircraft, and on 3 November he scored his fourth kill – success which saw him awarded the *Medaglia d'Argento al Valore Militare.*

'Il Piccinin' ('Kid'), as the youthful Lombardi was also called, 'made ace' on 4 November, although the date of his sixth kill remains unknown. In December, he flew reconnaissance sorties deep (up to 100 kilometres) into enemy territory, for which he received a second *Medaglia d'Argento.*

Switching to the SPAD VII in 1918, Tenente Lombardi did not score again until the Battle of the Piave in June, during which he was embroiled in a flurry of activity. On 15 June, the ace was credited with an Albatros D III, which he described as being red with white crosses and a black hand insignia, south of Biagio. The following day he downed Oeffag Albatros D III 153.222, flown by Leutnant der Reserve Hans Wolfschütz of *Flik* (*Fliegerkompagnie*) 41J, bringing his official total to eight.

After the war, 'Francis' Lombardi returned to his family's rice refinery, although he remained active in sports flying, and founded the *Vercelli Gruppo Turismo Aereo* in 1928. In 1930, he gained international attention with a series of long-distance flights in a Fiat AS.1 monoplane – one from Rome to Mogadishu, in Italian Somaliland, another from Vercelli to Tokyo, Japan and finally a circuit of the African coast. In 1938, he also formed the aircraft manufacturer Avia, whose L.3 two-seater became a common sight in military schools and flying clubs.

In 1976, the Italian Air Force awarded Lombardi a Gold Medal for Aeronautical Valour for his lifetime of aerial achievements, and in November 1981 he made the news for the last time when he attended the last reunion of World War 1 aces in Paris as the sole Italian representative. There, in contrast to the reserved cordiality of Austrian naval ace Gottfried Freiherr von Banfield and Canadian-Italian front aces Thomas F Williams and Gerald A Birks, Lombardi indulged in much emotional embracing with former Hungarian opponents Antal von Boksay, Hugo Maczenauer and István Piantovszki.

Francis Lombardi published an article on the airmen he had known during the war for the British *Cross & Cockade Society* just prior to his death in Vercelli on 5 March 1983. One of those he mentioned was his squadronmate, Ernesto Cabruna;

'I think people are born with a vocation to be *Carabinieri* (*gendarme*), and they usually have the build for it too – a stiff, unbending, body. They are morally rigid and inflexible too. This is how it was with Marechiallo dei Carabinieri Ernesto Cabruna. A sergeant in the infantry is nothing very much, but a sergeant

76ª Squadriglia's **Tenente Flavio Torello Baracchini evaluated this SPAD VII, which had been temporarily issued to his unit, in the summer of 1917. The fighter was not accepted by the squadron, however, and Baracchini gained all four of his confirmed and one probable victories scored whilst flying with *76ª* at the controls of a Hanriot HD 1. Wounded in action on 8 August, Baracchini returned to his previous unit – *81ª Squadriglia* – in March 1918, and duly scored a further nine victories in Hanriots prior to being wounded again on 25 June. His final official wartime tally was 21 kills** (*via Roberto Gentilli*)

Francesco Lombardi stands beside one of his SPAD VIIs, its fuselage marked with the red heart emblem of *77ª Squadriglia*, as well as the Italian cockade. Lombardi scored all eight of his victories with *77ª*, making him the squadron's leading ace. He gained further renown in 1930 for three long-range flights from Rome to Mogadishu, Vercelli to Tokyo and a round-flight of Africa (*via Roberto Gentilli*)

of *Carabinieri* has authority – he makes himself felt. Cabruna had authority in the air too. He made himself felt – he was very "regimental", all spit-and-polish.'

Cabruna was born in Tortona, in Alessandria province, on 2 June 1889, and his SPAD VII carried his hometown's coat of arms aft of *77ª's* red heart unit insignia. He had joined the *Carabinieri Reali*, who served as both military and civilian policemen, in 1907. On 15 May 1916, while serving in Asiago, Cabruna rescued victims of an Austrian bombing raid, and he was subsequently awarded the *Medaglia di Bronzo* for his bravery. Two months later he began flight training at Torino, and received his flying licences on 6 October and 16 November.

Cabruna joined *28ª Squadriglia* on 28 December, and after further training in Nieuport fighters he went on to serve with both *84ª* and *80ª Squadriglie*. While with the latter unit, he scored his first two kills on 26 October and 5 December 1917, and was awarded the *Medaglia d'Argento*.

On 26 January 1918 Cabruna was transferred once more, this time to SPAD VII-equipped *77ª Squadriglia*, and it was in the French fighter that

This composite photographic postcard shows Sottotenente Ernesto Cabruna's SPAD VII S1420 of *77ª Squadriglia*, which can still be seen at the Italian Air Force Museum at Vigna di Valle, near Rome. By the end of the war, the Roman numerals 'XIII' had been stencilled on the upper wings, and nine crosses added to the fuselage upper decking, although only eight were confirmed by a post-war review committee (*via Roberto Gentilli*)

COMANDANTE

he was truly able to manifest his hard-nosed personality in aerial terms. He downed an aeroplane on 12 March, and his fourth victory was achieved during a lone patrol some 17 days later, when he encountered 11 Austro-Hungarian fighters. Lombardi later recalled;

'Without hesitation Cabruna dived right into the middle of them, firing bursts in every direction. He emerged unharmed, having shot one of them down. For this exploit he was awarded the *Medaglia d'Oro por Valore Militare*.'

Sergente Maggiore Aldo Bocchese of *70ª Squadriglia* perches on the cockpit sill of a SPAD VII that bears an unusual white personal marking. Having initially flown SAML two-seaters in 1917, Bocchese trained in fighters and opened his account with *70ª* by claiming a 'hat trick' of kills over Valdobbiadene on 17 April 1917. He shared in the downing of a two-seater and two fighters with Tenenti Flaminio Avet and Leopoldo Eleuteri and Sottotenente Alessandro Resch. His final wartime total came to six victories (*via Aaron Weaver*)

Cabruna became an ace on 15 June when he took on 30 enemy aeroplanes and brought down one of them. He downed another adversary five days later and shared in the destruction of a balloon on 21 June.

The ace broke his collarbone during a landing accident in Ansaldo A.1 No6548 on 26 September 1918, and although not fully recovered from his injury, Cabruna had returned by 25 October in order to participate in the final Italian offensive at Vittorio Veneto. He duly downed his eighth kill during the course of the day, as well as probably destroying a ninth aircraft later in the same mission. And although this ninth victory could not be confirmed, Cabruna indicated that he thought otherwise by painting nine crosses on the fuselage upper decking of his SPAD (S1420). On 2 November he strafed Aiello airfield, destroying two Austro-Hungarian aeroplanes on the ground.

Although he served for a time in the post-war *Regia Aeronautica*, and attained the rank of capitano and aide-de-camp to the Chief of Staff, Cabruna did not fit in well with the peacetime organisation, and he was discharged on 2 June 1932. He died in Rapello on 9 January 1960, but his SPAD VII survives, currently on display in the Italian Air Force Museum at Vigna di Valle, near Rome.

Italy's most renowned fighter unit, *91ª Squadriglia*, was formed on 1 May 1917 with an initial complement of four SPAD VIIs and three Nieuports. Led by Maggiore Guido Tacchini, the unit had at its heart a cadre of pilots drawn from *70ª Squadriglia* – these men were some of the most experienced aviators then serving in the *Aviazione del Regio Esercito*.

Most prominent among them was Capitano Francesco Baracca, who had scored Italy's first official aerial victory, in a Nieuport 11, on 7 April 1916. Known for decorating his Nieuport 17 with a black prancing stallion in memory of his old cavalry unit, *11º Regimento Piemonte Reale*, Baracca's score had risen to eight by the time he joined *91ª Squadriglia*.

Given command of the unit in June 1917, Baracca, like Germany's Manfred von Richthofen and France's Félix Brocard, began actively seeking out talented pilots to form a 'squadron of aces'. Among them were Pier Ruggero Piccio, who would eventually become Italy's second-ranking ace with 24 victories, Fulco Ruffo di Calabria (21 victories), Ferruccio Ranza (17), Gastone Novelli (8), Luigi Olivari (8) Giuliano Parvis (6) Guido Nardini (6) and Giovanni Sabelli (5). Also in similar fashion to Richthofen, Baracca gave his pilots plenty of leeway in the air, trusting in their ability to know when to fight as a team or to hunt alone.

The individuality of Baracca's paladins was reflected in the personal markings that adorned the fuselages of their Nieuport and SPAD fighters. Piccio had a black flag and Ruffo a black skull and crossbones, while Ranza and Sabelli had ladder-like motifs. Giuliano Parvis, an Italian Irredentist from Austrian-held Trieste who had adopted a pseudonym in place of his real name of Giorgio Pessi, and claimed Rome as his birthplace in hopes of avoiding being shot as a traitor should he fall in enemy hands, used a crescent as his personal heraldry.

By the end of *91ª*'s first month in action, its pilots had accounted for 14 Austro-Hungarian aircraft, including two by Baracca in a Nieuport on 1 and 10 May, his first victory in a SPAD VII (over a Brandenburg C I) on 13 May, and another Brandenburg on 20 May. Piccio, who had opened his account while serving in *77ª Squadriglia* by burning a balloon on 18 October 1916, added Albatroses to his tally on 20 and 28 May 1917, and forced an aeroplane down on 1 June. Sottotenente Olivari also added to the carnage with an Albatros on 18 May and Lohner flying boat L136 (the crew of which were wounded and taken prisoner) on 24 May.

91ª was transferred to Istrana airfield to support operations in the Trentino sector on 6 June. On that same day Olivari, who had scored his seventh victory on 3 June, downed Brandenburg C I 229.19 between Monte Santo and Gargaro, killing its crew. On 23 June, Tenente Ferruccio Ranza (with four kills to his name from his time with *77ª Squadriglia* in 1916) 'made ace' by downing an enemy two-seater between Valsugana and Barco. By the time *91ª* returned to Santa Caterina on 29 June, its reputation was made, and it became known as the '*Squadriglia degli Assi*'.

When the Italians launched a new offensive along the Isonzo River on 18 August 1917, *71ª, 75ª, 76ª, 77ª, 78ª* and *91ª Squadriglie* had at least some SPAD VIIs on strength, and these units were joined in October by *72ª, 80ª* and *84ª Squadriglie*. Among their principal opposition in the air was *Flik* 41j, whose commander, Hptm Godwin Brumowski, had groomed his unit into an Austro-Hungarian 'squadron of aces' after returning from a visit to German *Jagdstaffeln* on the Western Front, including the Richthofen Circus.

Brumowski himself was credited with 12 victories in 16 days during the battle, while Baracca added enemy two-seaters to his score on 19 August and 1 September, and teamed up with Sabelli to bring down a Brandenburg C I of *Flik* 34 on 6 September – this was the latter pilot's second kill. A Neopolitan, Sabelli had earned Royal Aero Club licence No 178 at Brooklands, England, on 30 January 1912, and had then allegedly helped organise the Bulgarian Air Service to fight the Turks later that year.

He added three more aeroplanes to his tally on 17, 23 and 29 September, earning him his second wartime *Medaglia d'Argento*. *91ª* suffered a saddening loss on 13 October 1917, however, when Tenente Olivari was killed when his SPAD VII stalled and crashed while taking off.

The costly 11th Battle of the Isonzo advanced the Italian lines only five miles, and as the Italians were poised for a renewed effort on 24 October, they suddenly found themselves the target of an Austro-Hungarian offensive, bolstered by German troops and 90 German aircraft. Three days before the disastrous Battle of Caporetto, Baracca had experienced his first

Capitano Francesco Baracca stands beside the SPAD VII in which he scored his 11th victory on 13 May 1917 – and 18 more thereafter. When SPAD XIIIs arrived at *91ª Squadriglia* in late November, Baracca was hesitant to abandon the nimbler SPAD VII. 'It doesn't matter if the VII is equipped with a single gun', he remarked. 'Provided you are a good fighter, a single gun is just enough'

Third-ranking among Italy's aces, Tenente Colonello Pier Ruggero Piccio scored at least ten victories in Nieuports and increased his total to 24 in SPADs, which he reportedly decorated with a black flag as a personal marking

Seen wearing his flying helmet, *91ª Squadriglia's* Tenente Giorgio Pessi – aka Giuliano Parvis – prepares to climb aboard his crescent-marked SPAD VII (S1714). Pessi claimed eight victories (only six were confirmed by a post-war review committee) before transferring to the *Commissariato generale d'Aeronautica* on 16 March 1918. Joining the airline Aero Espresso Italiana in the 1920s, he was lost at sea in a Dornier Wal while en route to the Isle of Rhodes on 18 July 1933 (*via Aaron Weaver*)

Yet another paladin of Baracca's *91ª Squadriglia* was Tenente Ferruccio Ranza, who scored four victories in Nieuport 11s with *77ª Squadriglia*, before transferring to *91ª* in early June 1917 and bringing his total to 17 by 17 August 1918. He is shown here after the war still flying a SPAD VII, the veteran fighter remaining in Italian service into the 1920s

combat in a new SPAD XIII (on 21 October), during which he shot down two enemy two-seaters. One fell at Ravne, behind Italian lines, and its crew turned out to be German (Ltns Arthur Fischer and Heinrich Hansberg of *Fl. Abt.* 14). Baracca's first double haul had also been his first over German aircraft.

'On the 25th, there was great activity', Baracca wrote. 'I had five fights with the Germans. At 1100 I shot down an Austrian Albatros over San Marco (Gorizia) with Tenente Colonello Piccio. In the evening, I had my SPAD shot up and its longeron broken into pieces by enemy machine-gun fire in an aerial dogfight.

'Two of my pilots fell during the fighting', he continued. 'Sabelli, downed in flames and Tenente Ferreri shot down by enemy fighters over Tolmino. Ruffo shot down two enemies in flames and Piccio another one in flames over Cividale. We claimed six aeroplanes in all.'

Baracca and Piccio's first victim was from *Flik* 19, the crew, Feldwebel Anton Lambert and Ltn Johann Poppius, being killed. In addition to the two victories that Baracca witnessed, Ruffo was credited with a third that day, shared with Capitano 'Bortolo' Constantini (the latter's first of an eventual six kills). Ranza also downed a DFW C V of *Fl. Abt.* 39 over Lom.

Ferreri had been killed by Ltn Herbert Schroeder of German *Jasta* 1, while Sabelli was reportedly downed while he and Piccio were engaging a two-seater. However, the Austrians credited him as the eighth of an eventual 28 kills for Viennese Oblt Benno Fiala Ritter von Fernbrugg, then serving in *Flik* 12D. It is possible that the Austrians erroneously associated the remains of Sabelli's aeroplane with Fiala's claim, which may in fact have been over Baracca, whose SPAD was shot-up but not shot down.

On 26 October Baracca and Parvis downed two German DFW C Vs in flames, while Constantini destroyed an Aviatik two-seater. On the ground, meanwhile, Caporetto became a disastrous Italian rout, with 275,000 prisoners being taken by the forces of the Central Powers. The surviving Italians retreated past the Tagliamento River on 2 November.

By then *91ª Squadriglia's* SPADs were so worn out that its pilots had to fly Nieuport 17s and Hanriot HD 1s until the first week of November, when the unit withdrew from Pordenone to Padowa aerodrome. New SPADs soon arrived, and the unit returned to action, literally with a vengeance, on 6 November. Late that morning, Baracca and Parvis encountered two Oeffag-Albatros D IIIs of *Flik* 41J whilst on a patrol.

'The one engaged by Parvis, after a short fight, fled toward Latisana', Baracca reported. 'Mine, alarmed by my attack, continued to escape, going down in spirals. I fired short bursts until we were just 50 metres above the trees, with me continually harassing my foe from close behind until the enemy stalled and crashed into the ground.'

Baracca's Hungarian opponent, Oblt Rudolf Szepessy-Sököll Freiherr von Négyes és Rénö, had scored his fourth and fifth victories over two Macchi L-3 flying boats just 24 hours earlier. Hit in the spine, he

Tenente Giovanni Sabelli's SPAD VII sported a smaller variation on fellow *91ª Squadriglia* ace Ferruccio Ranza's ladder motif, with this particular rendition being applied in red. Born in Naples, Sabelli earned his civil Royal Aero Club licence at Brooklands, in England, on 30 January 1912, and he later helped organise the Bulgarian Air Service during the nation's war against Turkey. After serving in Italy and Albania, he joined *91ª Squadriglia* on 23 June 1917 and was credited with five victories between 10 August and 29 September. Sabelli was killed on 25 October, however, when his fighter was shot down in flames by a two-seater (*via Aaron Weaver*)

managed to glide his D III (153.54) back over the frontline, before crash-landing near Latisana. Despite his efforts, he died as he was being lifted from the cockpit. Parvis' adversary, Feldwebel Radames Iskra, force-landed his D III (153.08) at Treviso and was swiftly taken prisoner. But the two Italians had not yet finished their patrol.

'After a short while, we met two German reconnaissance aircraft at about 3400 metres', Parvis wrote in his combat report. 'While we were getting closer, I saw two enemy fighters, which were coming to the rescue of their two-seaters, about 300 metres below us. I kept my eyes on the fighters, while Maggiore Baracca attacked one of the two-seaters. Then, I dived toward the latter . . . I fired a few shots, the two-seater went into a spin first and then crashed near Codega.'

Parvis' victim had been a DFW C V of *Fl. Abt.* 219, and its crew, Vfw Werner Schroeder and Ltn Albrecht Binder, were killed. The Baracca and Parvis team downed another C V near Orsago the next day, after which Baracca strafed the wreck and set it alight. Again the crew (Gefreiter Wil-

After scoring eight victories in Nieuports with *70ª* and *91ª Squadriglie*, Capitano Fulco Ruffo di Calabria downed another dozen enemy aircraft in SPADs. All of his fighters were marked with variations of the skull and crossbones motif (*via Greg VanWyngarden*)

helm Appelt and Ltn Paul Wilkening of *Fl. Abt. (A)* 204) were killed.

Baracca downed yet another of *Fl.Abt.14's* machines in flames on 15 November, and eight days later he and Novelli sent an Albatros scout crashing near Vidor, killing Vfw Karl Überschär of *Jasta* 39.

Although the past month had been a fiasco for their army, Baracca and his '*Squadriglia degli Assi'* had more than upheld Italian honour over Caporetto, proving themselves able to match not only the best men and machines that Austria-Hungary could throw at them, but Germany as well.

By 10 November the Italians had taken up new defensive positions

south of the Piave River, and the front stabilised. Later that month, SPAD XIIIs began arriving in quantity at *91ª Squadriglia*, although Baracca was not terribly impressed with them. 'It doesn't matter if the VII is equipped with a single gun', he opined. 'Provided you are a good fighter, a single gun is just enough'.

Although *77ª* and *91ª Squadriglie's* pilots did well in SPADs, most Italian airmen preferred the manoeuvrability of the Nieuport 17 and the Hanriot HD 1 to the SPAD 's speed, which they regarded as more useful for a high-speed reconnaissance aeroplane.

Another factor against the SPAD in Italian service was the fact that Macchi had obtained a licence to manufacture the HD 1, whereas France was straining to supply SPADs to all her allies. Consequently, in November 1917, HD 1s replaced the SPAD VIIs of *76ª*, *80ª* and *84ª Squadriglie*. By June 1918, *91ª Squadriglia* was entirely equipped with the SPAD XIII, but as with some French *escadrilles*, SPAD VIIs served on in a handful of Italian units right up until the end of the war.

Russian Aces

The first Russian to achieve success in the SPAD VII did so over the Western Front. Nobleman Ivan Aleksandrovich Orlov from St Petersburg (who had designed a powered aeroplane in 1913) scored his first three victories in Nieuport 11s while leading the 7th Fighter Detachment in Galicia in 1916. He was then sent to France, where he was temporarily assigned to *Escadrille* N3 in order to study fighter tactics under such masters as Georges Guynemer and Alfred Heurtaux. Flying one of the *escadrille's* SPADs, he demonstrated what he had learned by shooting down a German aircraft on 24 January 1917.

Returning to Russia and rejoining the 7th Detachment in March, Orlov downed an Albatros of *Fl.*

And here are examples of the skull and crossbones insignia that Capitano Fulco Ruffo di Calabria applied to his SPAD VIIs whilst serving with *91ª Squadriglie* (*both via Aaron Weaver*)

91ª Squadriglia's **17-kill ace Ferruccio Ranza sits alongside his black ladder-marked SPAD VII. This insignia was the inspiration for the marking applied to squadronmate Tenente Giovanni Sabelli's SPAD VII, as seen on page 71 (*via Aaron Weaver*)**

Abt. (A) 242 for his fifth victory while flying a Nieuport 17 on 21 May, but he was subsequently killed in action on 4 July 1917.

By early 1917, 43 SPAD VIIs had been delivered to the Imperial Russian Air Service, and the Aktionyernoye Obschchestovo Dux plant in Moscow had been contracted to build a further 200. It had only completed about half that number, however, when shortages of Hispano-Suiza engines caused the order to be terminated in early 1918. SPAD VIIs were allotted to several squadrons, but most were sent to the 1st Fighter Group, comprised of the II, IV, XI and XIX Corps Fighter Detachments, which under the command of Rotmistre (cavalry captain) Aleksandr A Kozakov had established itself as the premier fighter unit in the Imperial Russian Air Service (IRAS).

Born in Kherson on 15 January 1889, Aleksandr Aleskandrovich Kozakov had been an officer of the 12th Belgorod Uhlan Cavalry Regiment in 1908, but had transferred to aviation in 1913. One of the pioneer fighter pilots of the IRAS, he scored his first victory on 31 March 1915, by ramming an enemy two-seater after unsuccessfully trying to destroy its rigging with an anchor dragged from his Morane-Saulnier G monoplane! He scored two more victories in June and July 1916, using a Nieuport 10 armed with an obliquely-mounted Maxim machine gun, before settling on the Nieuport 11 and 17 as his aerial weapons of choice.

SPAD VIIs began to arrive at the 1st Fighter Group in the summer of 1917. Kozakov decorated his own machine with a black skull and crossbones on a white rudder (the reversed colours of his former unit, the XIX Detachment), as well as cowl stripes that have been variously described as dark blue and gold, in reference to his former cavalry unit, or red and blue. Although he flew this fighter on several occasions, he preferred his older, but combat-proven, Nieuport 17, and his SPAD was more often flown by his deputy, Esaul (Cossack captain) Shangin.

On 27 July 1917, Kozakov in his Nieuport and Shangin in the SPAD downed Austro-Hungarian Brandenburg C I 26.27 of *Flik* 20 over Obertyn, the crew being taken prisoner. The two Russians teamed up again on 2 August to shoot down Brandenburg C I 62.67 of *Flik* 26 over Hotyn. Its pilot, Cpl Traian Varzanon, crash-landed his aircraft near Dolinyany and later died of his wounds, while his officer observer, Franz Slivik, was taken prisoner.

At that point, Kozakov's score stood at 15, and he had raised it to 18 by 11 September, when he brought down a Brandenburg of *Flik* 18 near Kutkovez, its slightly wounded crewmen being taken prisoner. The following day, Kozakov and Shangin encountered four

Below
Two SPAD VIIs assigned to the Imperial Russian Air Service in 1917. The fighter in the foreground has a Russian cockade (red, blue and white) on its rudder, while the other machine was assigned to Stabs-Kapitan Aleksandr A Kozakov, commander of the 1st Combat Air Group

Bottom
Kozakov's SPAD VII bore a black skull and crossbones on a white rudder. Its cowl stripes have been variously described as dark blue and gold, in reference to Kozakov's former cavalry unit, or red and blue. In any case, Kozakov scored no victories with this machine, often letting his deputy, Esaul (Cossack Captain) Shangin fly the SPAD while he stuck to his tried and tested Nieuport 17

Austro-Hungarian aircraft, and Shangin succeeded in forcing one of them down before he too crash-landed in enemy territory after being set upon by the remaining fighters. He was quickly captured. Meanwhile, an enraged Kozakov hurled his Nieuport at the remaining aircraft and ultimately drove them back toward their aerodrome.

Kozakov, who became the Russian ace of aces, only to be mortally injured in an air crash on 1 August 1919 while commanding the Slavo-British flying detachment during the Russian Civil War, scored none of his 20 victories in the SPAD VII, although several of his pilots did.

Most prominent among them was Praporshik (ensign) Ivan Vasilievich Smirnov. Born to a farming family in Vladimir on 30 January 1895, Ivan Smirnov enlisted in the 96th Omsk Regiment when World War 1 broke out. After being wounded in the leg on 8 December 1914, he decided to transfer to aviation, and by August 1916 he was serving in Kozakov's XIX Corps Fighter Detachment.

Stabs-Rotmistre (cavalry staff captain) Kozakov (second from top) and officers of the XIX Detachment, 1st Combat Air Group, are seen in Stanislav, Romania, in February or March 1917. Amongst these pilots are Praporshik (ensign) Longin Lipsky (front row, extreme left), Starski Unteroffizier (sergeant) Ivan V Smirnov (front row, third from left), Stabs-Kapitan Pavel V Argeyev (front row, fourth from left) and Praporshik Ernst K Leman (front row, second from right). Born in Lithuania in 1894, Leman had scored five victories by the time he attempted suicide on 17 December 1917 following the Bolshevik Revolution. He died of his self-inflicted head wound several days later

Smirnov scored his first victory flying a two-seat Nieuport 10 on 2 January 1917, and his next four kills were achieved in Morane-Saulnier I and Nieuport 17 scouts, before he received a SPAD VII in early September 1917. He was flying the new type over the village of Balin on the 24th when he and Praporshik Longin Lipsky spotted a German Albatros C III of *Fl. Abt. (A)* 240. Diving down to attack it, their bullets mortally wounded the observer, Lt d R Paul Thierfelder, who was struck in the head. At that point the pilot, Uffz Paul Utsch, chose the better part of valour and landed his slightly damaged aeroplane behind Russian lines. This sixth kill saw Smirnov awarded the Golden Sword of St George.

After several frustrating bouts with a jammed machine gun, Smirnov downed an aeroplane from *Fl. Abt. (A)* 283 over Kovel on 23 October, killing its pilot, Gefreiter Helmut Tehsenvitz.

Over the next few weeks, the tenuous control of Gen Aleksandr Kerensky's Provisional Government over Russia broke down, and on 8 November, the Bolsheviks issued a peace decree. Soldiers were urged to cease fighting the Germans and encouraged to kill their officers if they insisted otherwise. Smirnov and Lipsky expressed their opinion of this daunting situation on 11 November, when they took off to intercept two Brandenburg C Is of *Flik* 9 that were photographing the Russian trenches. The motor of Lipsky's Nieuport 21 failed, but Smirnov proceeded on in his SPAD and quickly sent C I 269.08 down in flames to crash-land and roll over, spilling its crewmen (who were lucky under the circumstances) to the ground seconds before it crashed into the trench wire near Zelena. As Smirnov turned to deal with the second aeroplane, he reported that his machine gun jammed;

'I could only circle over it, and it would be crazy for me to attack it being armed only with my revolver. Suddenly I saw Lipsky. I continued to distract the attention of the German (sic) circling around so that Lipsky could approach me unnoticed. Before the German realised what was going on, Lipsky dove firing a whirlwind of bullets at him. The German caught fire fast and went down following his comrade.'

Esaul Shangin's SPAD VII is seen being manhandled by Austro-Hungarian troops soon after it was brought down on 12 September 1917. Its pilot was taken prisoner

The crewmen of Brandenburg C I 269.68, Josef Ryba and Josef Barcal, crashed to their deaths south of Zelena, and were jointly credited to Smirnov and Lipsky.

Smirnov struck again on 23 November, getting into a vicious gun duel with a Lloyd C V of *Flik* 18 that ended when he killed both crewmen and sent it crashing south of Letovo. Teaming up with Kozakov on 26 November, Smirnov attacked four enemy aeroplanes in the Skolat region, and the two aces sent one crashing behind enemy lines for Kozakov's 20th and Smirnov's 11th victory. Afterward, Gen Vyacheslav Tkachev, commander in chief of the IRAS, sent a telegram to the XIX Corps Fighter Detachment praising Smirnov, and declaring;

'During the days of terrible devastation and deathly danger for our long suffering country, your actions insure us that our glorious pilots will fulfil to the end their duty, and they would remain at their difficult, but glorious posts, winning new crowns of laurels from our fine native aviation.'

Encouraging though such a message was, it also brought Smirnov to the attention of the Bolsheviks, who marked him for assassination. Catching wind of the plot, Smirnov, Lipsky and another pilot deserted their unit and got out of Russia in early 1918.

Smirnov turned up as assistant air attaché and chief test pilot for the White Russians in Paris, then as a member of the Slavonic-British aviation detachment during the Russian Civil War. After the Bolshevik victory, he served in the RAF as an instructor at Upavon and Netheravon aerodromes. In 1920, he joined the Belgian airline SNETA, then flew for Royal Dutch Airlines (KLM) after 1922. Whilst fly a DC-3, he was shot down and wounded off Broome, Western Australia, by three Mitsubishi A6M2 Zeros on 2 March 1942. Despite this brush with death, Smirnov kept flying for KLM until 1949, and died in Majorca in October 1956.

At least two other Russian aces, both serving in the IX Fighter Detachment, are known to have flown SPAD VIIs with success. Praporshik Vladimir I Strizhevsky used one to down a Brandenburg D I on 17 May 1917 and a Fokker E III on 17 June for his fifth and sixth out of a total of seven victories. Praporshik Grigori E Suk, who had scored three victories in Nieuport 11s and two in a Vickers FB 19, brought his total to

One of the earliest military pilots in the IRAS, Aleksandr Aleksandrovich Kozakov attacked the enemy with everything from anchors to machine guns, flying Morane-Saulnier monoplanes and Nieuport 10s and 17s. Credited with 20 victories, he was Russia's leading ace of World War 1. Having survived the Great War, he was mortally injured on 1 August 1919 when his Sopwith Snipe crashed while fighting the Bolsheviks during the Russian Civil War. He died of his injuries three days later

This SPAD VII was flown by Praporshik Ivan Vasilievich Smirnov of XIX Detachment, 1st Combat Air Group, during the summer of 1917. Undaunted by the deteriorating situation in Russia, Smirnov scored seven victories in this fighter (*via Johan Visser*)

Georges Marcel Lachmann may not have been one of the highest-scoring French aces, but he may have been the most peripatetic, serving on the Western Front in 1914, the Italian Front with the *Escadrille Nieuport de Mestre* in Venice from August 1915 to February 1916, with N57 at Verdun (where he scored his first two victories) and then with N581 in Russia

nine in a SPAD VII between 14 October and 10 November 1917. He was also killed in the aeroplane, however, while coming in to land at his airfield on 28 November.

Given the fact that some Russian aces flew SPADs in France, perhaps it was fitting that two French SPAD aces added to their scores in Russia. In February 1917, the French dispatched two *escadrilles*, Sop582 equipped with Sopwith 1.A2 reconnaissance aircraft and N581 with Nieuport 17s and SPAD VII fighters, to Russia. On 27 May, the units were attached to the Russian Seventh Army and served alongside Kozakov's 1st Fighter Group during the Russian offensive in Galicia throughout June, as well as the German counteroffensive between 21 July and 11 August. After that, N581 was transferred to the Russian III Corps.

Born in Paris on 10 August 1890, N581's top-scoring pilot, Sous-Lt Georges Marcel Lachmann, had already seen service over the Western Front in several *escadrilles*, and over Italy with N92 by the end of 1915. Returning to France for service in N57, he destroyed a balloon and two German aircraft between 15 July and 12 August 1916. He was transferred to Russia in January 1917, and assigned to N581 on 21 March. On the night of 26 June, Lachmann tried to carry out a surprise nocturnal attack on a grounded German balloon, but upon his return he misjudged where to land and ended up crashing into some trees. Lachmann had barely recovered from his injuries when he became N581's CO on 8 July.

On 1 September, he reported that he penetrated enemy territory and spotted a 'Boche sausage' 12 kilometres behind the frontline;

'I returned to land at the field to get my rockets and left again. At the moment I arrived over the lines (the balloon) was at 1800 metres. I dove on it as best I could, and in spite of its extreme speed of descent I caught up with it at 500 metres. Of my six rockets, only one launched! I fired so close that my wheels weren't more than a metre away from it. It caught fire, and two observers jumped by parachute. Strongly machine-gunned and cannonaded at very close range, I passed over the lines at 800 metres.'

Lachmann claimed his fifth victory, a German two-seater which fell into Russian territory at Chilovtsi, on 18 September, followed by another over Malistoni on 3 October. Five days later, Lachmann teamed up with Sous-Lt Louis Coudouret to bring down an Albatros two-seater.

Although credited with a total of seven victories on both fronts, Lachmann was also alleged to have burned a balloon over Melnitza on 19 October. In addition to being made a *Chevalier de la Légion d'Honneur*, and receiving the *Croix de Guerre* with ten *Palmes*, he was also awarded the Italian *Croce da Guerra* and made a Knight of the Crown of Italy. He was also presented with the Russian Order of St George.

After the war, the ever-peripatetic Georges Lachmann travelled to Africa, carrying out research and reconnaissance missions to find new airfield locations. He died at Tonnerre on 12 August 1961.

N581's other leading light, Louis Fernand Coudouret, was born in Marseilles on 31 May 1896. He had seen previous service in VB102 and, like Lachmann, in N57, with whom he downed an LVG two-seater on 4 May 1916. Coudouret then transferred to N112 and N102, being credited with a second aeroplane while in the latter unit, on 22 October 1916.

When the call came for volunteers to go to Russia Coudouret responded, and he departed France on 22 March 1917, arriving in Moscow on 15 April. After scoring his third victory on 8 October, he brought down a Rumpler two-seater behind Russian lines on 23 November, its crew, Vfw Wilhelm Krauser and Lt d R Paul Strathmann of *Fl. Abt.(A) 232*, being taken prisoner.

Five days later, the Bolsheviks declared an armistice, but it was torrential rains, rather than the armistice, which restricted French aerial activity until 1 December. Late in the day, a brief break in the weather allowed Coudouret to fly a patrol, during which he encountered an Albatros D V and drove it down into German territory for his fifth victory.

There was little more that N581 could do at that point. After some tense months amid the power struggle developing following the Russian Revolution, the unit's personnel made their way to Murmansk, from whence they embarked for home on 15 March.

Returning to France on 1 April 1918, Coudouret was assigned to SPA103 on 18 May. On 2 June, he scored his sixth kill by sharing in the destruction of a fighter over Carlepont with an American LFC squadron-mate, Sgt Robert B Hoeber. In 1929, Coudouret planned to make an east-to-west transatlantic crossing, but while test-flying his Bernard aeroplane on 7 July, he crashed and was killed at Ageau, near Angoulême.

American Aces

The French sold a total of 189 SPAD VIIs to the United States. By the time deliveries began in December 1917, however, a number of Americans had already flown the type in combat – as volunteers who had entered French service through the Foreign Legion.

The first such pilots formed a unit in April 1916, which was initially designated N124, but better known as the *Escadrille Américaine* until German diplomats protested about their presence to the government of the then neutral United States.

The unit was then to be redesignated the *Escadrille des Volontaires*, but its members considered that sobriquet too dull, and eventually replaced it with a reference to a Frenchman who had assisted their country during its war for independence – Maj-Gen Marie Joseph Paul Ives Gilbert du Motier, Marquis de Lafayette.

When the number of American volunteers exceeded the number of positions available within the *Escadrille Lafayette*, they were assigned to other French units by an organisation that came to be known as the *Lafayette* Flying Corps, or LFC.

Like Lachmann, Sous-Lt Louis Coudouret served in *Escadrille* N57 as well as N102, scoring a victory in each unit before being assigned to the French Aeronautic Mission to Russia. He claimed three victories in Russia with N581 and then returned to France, where he scored his sixth and final kill with SPA103

Russian officers examine Sous-Lt Lachmann's SPAD at Kamnietz-Padolsk airfield. In addition to the synchronised Vickers machine gun, Lachmann added a Lewis gun on a makeshift overwing mounting and occasionally Le Prieur rockets for balloon-busting missions. Three of his five successes in Russia were against balloons

The first SPAD VII reached N124 in October 1916, and by early June 1917 only two or three Nieuports remained within the unit. Its leading ace, Gervais Raoul Lufbery, scored most of his 16 victories in SPAD VIIs, and fellow ace Lt William Thaw was probably flying one when he shared in the destruction of an Albatros two-seater for his second kill on 26 April 1917. Sgt David McKelvey Peterson also reportedly flew one with a blue fuselage pennant aft of the *escadrille's* Sioux Indian head emblem to score his first victory over an Albatros D V on 19 September 1917.

Later serving in the United States Air Service (USAS), Peterson flew Nieuport 28s to score three victories in the 94th Aero Squadron, and two more in the 95th, all in May 1918. He attained the rank of major on 29 August, but was killed in a flying accident at Daytona Beach, Florida, on 16 March 1919.

Edwin Charles Parsons, who scored his first victory over a Rumpler C IV while flying a SPAD VII in SPA124 on 4 September 1917, noted;

'Our instruments were the crudest, and only the most essential. We had only a compass, a fairly reliable altimeter which showed us at least approximately our altitude from the field where we had taken off, a tachometer to show engine revolution, an oil pulsator to show oil was flowing, a clock and a map. That was the complete equipment.'

Unlike his squadronmates, Ted Parsons preferred to remain in French service when the *Lafayette Escadrille* transferred to the USAS in February 1918. After taking two months to go home on leave, he joined SPA3 in January 1918, and scored seven more victories with that famous unit.

On 18 February 1918, SPA124 underwent a metamorphosis that left it with something of a split personality. Its American personnel were transferred to the USAS and redesignated the 103rd Aero Squadron. Its commander, Maj Thaw, was also one of the founding fathers of the original N124, and had scored two victories while serving in it. SPA124, meanwhile, was re-formed as a French unit, although even then its personnel was not 100 per cent French – at least three Portuguese pilots were assigned to the unit, along with a Bohemian volunteer, Václav Pilat, and a Russian, Pavel Argeyev.

Both SPA124 and the 103rd Aero Squadron operated together from La Noblette aerodrome during the spring of 1918 as components of GC21, commanded by Capitaine Lucien Couret de Villeneuve. Also in the group were *escadrilles* SPA98, SPA157 and SPA163, whilst SPA164 joined later in the year.

As with GC12, whose SPADs were identified by the common theme of storks in various attitudes of flight, all of GC21's aircraft had diagonal fuselage bands of different colour combinations – yellow-black-yellow for SPA98, blue for SPA157, red-black-red for SPA163 and blue and red for SPA164. SPA124's SPAD VIIs had a white band and white numerals on the fuselage sides and starboard upper wing, and a large black number on the undersides of the port lower wing.

Among the first SPAD VIIs delivered to N124 was S156, which is seen here in front of Sgt Robert Soubiran's Nieuport 17 (N1977) in November 1916. In addition to the unit's Seminole Indian head, the fuselage was also marked with three red coup stripes forward of the tailplane and the butterfly marking of the *Escadrille's* French commander, Capitaine Georges Thénault. The early Seminole Indian unit insignia was based on the trademark that the Savage Arms Company applied to its boxes of ammunition. In April 1917, Sgt Edward Hinkle declared the Seminole head to be too bland, and he proposed a revised insignia featuring a fierce Sioux warrior wearing a larger war bonnet. The latter featured blue-tipped feathers, which in turn resulted in the headwear resembling a French tricolour from a distance (*SHAA B88.217 via Jon Guttman*)

Adjutant Gervais Raoul Lufbery strikes a characteristic pose beside a SPAD VII of SPA124 *Lafayette*. Born in Chamaliéres on 14 March 1885, Lufbery had a French mother, but his father was from Wallingford, Connecticut. A pre-war aviator, he joined the Foreign Legion, and following the death of his friend and flying mentor, Marc Pourpe, 'Luf' devoted himself to seeking revenge. His official score of 16 kills was the highest achieved by any American in French service during World War 1

SPAD VIIs and a lone Nieuport 24 await the day's patrol at SPA124's aerodrome at Chaudun in 1917. By the time this shot was taken, the Sioux head had replaced the Seminole as the *Escadrille* insignia, while individual aircraft were marked with personal motifs, rather than numerals (*SHAA B88.1115 via Jon Guttman*)

Following the squadron's distinguished participation in the defence of Reims at the end of May 1918, SPA124's commander, Capitaine André d'Humiéres, authorised the addition of the head of Joan of Arc (based on a statue in front of the cathedral of Frémiet) over the unit's white band. In contrast to its sister units in GC21, the 103rd Aero Squadron also 'inherited' the Sioux Indian head that its aircraft had worn in its *Escadrille Lafayette* days, as well as the use of personal motifs, rather than numbers, for individual identification.

In addition to the 103rd Aero Squadron's pilots, numerous Americans flew in other units in GC21. Some were *Lafayette* Flying Corps members who had transferred to the USAS but continued to serve with the French, others were USAS pilots who were farmed out to the French to gain combat experience until American squadrons could be organised for them, and a few were LFC personnel who preferred to remain in the *Aviation Française*. In the cases of SPA157 and 163, their only aces were American.

Hailing from Philadelphia, Pennsylvania, James Alexander Connelly, Jr joined SPA157 on 15 January 1918. His first victory was a balloon shared with fellow LFC member Sgt Sereno Thorpe Jacob on 20 April, followed by the shared destruction of an enemy aeroplane on 5 June.

Transferring to SPA163 on 27 June, Connelly stayed there until the end of the war, mostly flying SPAD XIIIs to raise his tally to seven by 4 November. In addition to the *Médaille Militaire* and *Croix de Guerre*, he received the American Distinguished Service Cross, but his relentless aerial activities undermined his health, and at least partially accounting for his premature death in New York on 2 February 1944.

Also seeing his first action in SPA157, on 26 December 1917, was Sgt Thomas Ganz Cassady from Spencer, Indiana. Transferred to the 103rd Aero Squadron in February 1918, Cassady was commissioned as a first lieutenant in the USAS, but then assigned to SPA163 on 14 May. There he came into his stride, shooting down five enemy aeroplanes between 28 May and 15 August flying SPAD VIIs and XIIIs. On 8 September, Cassady was made a flight leader in the USAS's 28th Aero Squadron, with whom he was subsequently credited with another four victories.

Promoted to captain in March 1919, Cassady was awarded the DSC and Oak Leaf, the *Légion d'Honneur* and *Croix de Guerre* with three *Palmes* and one *étoile*, although the latter awards were not made until the end of his association with France. During World War 2, he served as the US naval attaché to Vichy France – and as a spy for the Office of Strategic Services, helping downed Allied airmen to escape from France and assisting in the planning for the invasion of southern France in August 1944. Cassady died of cancer in Lake Forest, Illinois, on 9 July 1972, aged 76.

Cassady's first victory with SPA163 – an LVG downed on 28 May 1918 – was shared with Cpl Dequeker and LFC volunteer 1Lt William Thomas Ponder, a native of Mangum, Oklahoma, who had obtained his brevet on 7 November 1917, and joined SPA67 in February 1918. Commissioned in the USAS on 27 February, and transferred to SPA163 on 12 May, 'Wild Bill' Ponder was credited with two more victories flying SPAD XIIIs, before being transferred to the 103rd Aero Squadron. Here, he accounted for three more German aircraft and was awarded the DSC 'for extraordinary heroism' on 23 October 1918. Promoted to captain on 14 May 1919, Ponder died of a heart ailment in Amarillo, Texas, on 27 February 1947.

Mechanics of SPA124 play with the *Escadrille*'s famous lion mascots, 'Whiskey' and 'Soda', beside Sgt Edward Hinkle's SPAD VII (*via Greg van Wyndgarden*)

Although SPA124 was reconstituted as a French *escadrille* after 18 February 1918, its roster included pilots from Portugal, Bohemia, Russia and one remaining American, 1Lt Henry B Marsh. The foreign pilots generally received SPAD VIIs with high numbers, and No 19 in this lineup was used by Russian volunteer Capitaine Pavel Argeyev to score the first two of his nine victories with the unit (*SHAA B87.3781 via Jon Guttman*)

Arguably the most renowned LFC ace after Lufbery was David Endicott Putnam, who was born in Jamaica Plains, Massachusetts, on 10 December 1898. His ancestry, which included Revolutionary War Gen Israel Putnam, lent a certain inevitability to his decision to join the French air service in April 1917 – but he was also motivated by the fact that the USAS had turned him down as underage.

Initially joining SPA94 in December 1917, he became part of the cadre of a newly-forming *escadrille* – N156 – on 1 January 1918. He scored two victories in Nieuports that month, after which the unit received Morane-Saulnier AI parasol fighters in February. A series of wing failures soon grounded the new aeroplanes pending their replacement with SPAD VIIs, but Putnam refused to let that stop him from seeing combat in the fast, nimble little parasols, and he claimed nine kills between 12 April and 15 May. Typically, the aggressive Putnam fought so far into enemy territory that only one of his claims (a Rumpler on 15 March) was confirmed.

On 1 June Putnam scored his first victory in a SPAD VII, and on the 2nd he transferred to SPA38, shooting down two Albatros scouts on that same day, and six enemy aeroplanes – of which one Albatros D V was

Pilots of SPA163 pose for a group photograph at Somme-Vesle in August 1918. Standing, from left to right, are Sgt Serge Lederlin, MdL Jean Morvan, Adj Alan A Cook, Brig Marsaux, MdL Edouard Fery, Sgt James A Connelly Jr, Sgt Marcel Guillet, MdL Robert le Roux and MdL Dequeker. Seated, from left to right, are Lt Auguste Cousin, 1Lt William T Ponder, Capt de Champagny, 1Lt Thomas G Cassady and Lt Chereau. Connelly scored two victories with SPA157 and five with SPA163, whilst 'Wild Bill' Ponder claimed three with SPA163 and a trio of kills with the USAS's 103rd Aero Squadron

confirmed – on 5 June. Honing his skills under the tutelage of Lt Georges Madon, Putnam made three more unconfirmed claims on 14 June, but on the following day he was credited with a two-seater and a balloon, bringing his score to nine.

Amid all that activity, Putnam was awarded the *Médaille Militaire* and *Croix de Guerre*, and on 10 June he was commissioned a first lieutenant in the 103rd Aero Squadron, USAS, even though he was still flying missions with SPA38. By the end of June, however, he was serving as a flight commander in the USAS's 39th Aero Squadron, and like his French mentor, Madon, sharing his experience with and inspiring a new generation of fighter pilots.

BAER AND THAW ACHIEVE ACEDOM

The most successful exponent of the SPAD VII in the USAS (in fact, the only American to become an ace exclusively in that type while serving in a USAS squadron), Paul Frank Baer had gained previous experience with the French as a member of the LFC. Born in Fort Wayne, Indiana, on 29 January 1895, Baer enlisted in the Foreign Legion on 20 February 1917. Transferring to aviation, he qualified as a pilot on 15 June, and on 14 August he was assigned to SPA80 at Souilly. At first issued with a Nieuport 24, Baer soon moved on to SPAD VII S2124, the rear fuselage of which he painted as if draped with an American flag.

Although he scored no victories with SPA80, the athletically-built and trained Baer was praised by squadronmates like seven-victory ace Robert Delannoy for his companionability, his energy and his steadfast reliability as a wingman.

Although *Lafayette* Flying Corps member Thomas G Cassady was transferred to the USAS, and commissioned as a first lieutenant, in February 1918, he was assigned to SPA163 from 14 May to 8 September 1918. Cassady scored five victories with this unit, before being posted to the 28th Aero Squadron as a flight leader, with whom he claimed a further four kills. During World War 2 Cassady worked for the French Resistance and the Office of Strategic Services

On 6 January 1918, Cpl Baer and a fellow American from SPA80, Charles Herbert Wilcox, were transferred to SPA124. However, before they could fly with the *Lafayette Escadrille*, it became the 103rd Aero Squadron (on 18 February).

On 11 March 1918, the experience Baer had accumulated with SPA80 began to bear fruit as he downed an Albatros over Cenay-les-Reims for his and the 103rd Aero Squadron's first confirmed victory. Five days later, he and Sous-Lt Levrier of SPA38 downed an Albatros two-seater over Nogent-l'Abesse.

The 103rd's third victory was a joint effort by three old members of its *Lafayette* forebear, namely Maj Thaw, Capt James Norman Hall and 1Lt Christopher W Ford, who downed a German scout near Somme-Py on 27 March. 'Jimmy' Hall then claimed a second enemy fighter over St Étienne-á-Arnes to raise his personal tally to three. Baer scored his third victory on 6 April, when he sent an enemy scout crashing near Somme-Py, killing Uffz Georg Erdmann of *Jasta* 73.

On 10 April GC21 moved up to Bonne Maison, near Fismes, to commence operations in earnest, joining French ground forces opposing the last great German offensive of the war. Two days later, Baer downed an Albatros over Proyart.

At 1812 hrs on 20 April, Bill Thaw and 1Lt George Evans Turnure (a former LFC pilot who had served in SPA103) teamed up to burn a kite balloon at Montaigu, and 15 minutes later Thaw sent an enemy scout down in flames over Reservoir-Merval, bringing his total to five. Three days later Baer and Wilcox shared in the destruction of an Albatros two-seater over St Gobain. This was a significant victory for both pilots, as it was Wilcox's first and Baer's fifth.

Whereas it had taken Bill Thaw (who had scored his first kill on 24 May 1916) almost two years to become an ace, Baer had achieved that status in less than a month-and-a-half! In all fairness to Thaw, however, it might be added that he had accomplished his successes in spite of his having 20/80 vision, a hearing defect and a knee injury that severely limited his agility.

Indeed, under ordinary circumstances, he would not have been allowed in the military at all, but by the time Thaw left the USAS, he was a lieutenant colonel, and had been awarded the Distinguished Service Cross with Oak Leaf Cluster, the *Croix de Guerre* with four *Palmes* and two stars, and had been made a *Chevalier de la Légion d'Honneur*.

On 30 April the 103rd Aero Squadron was detached from GC21 and dispatched to Bray Dunes to assist the British over Flanders. Eight days later Baer downed two opponents over Mount Kemmel – a two-seater, probably resulting in the deaths of Uffz Paul Fritz and Ltn Ulrich Haupt of *Fl. Abt.(A)* 240, and a fighter whose pilot survived. On 21 May, Baer and Wilcox joined 1Lts Chris Ford and Hobart A H Baker in bringing down an Albatros west of Ypres.

The following day Baer was leading 1st Lts Wilcox, Turnure, Ernest A Giroux and William Dugan on a patrol when they encountered five

1Lt Cassady teamed up with Sgts Guillet and Lederlin to bring down this Halberstadt CL II of *Schlachstaffel* 26 at Ferte Gaucher on 23 June 1918 – its crew was taken prisoner. The demise of this aircraft gave Cassady his third accredited victory

One of the legendary aces of the *Lafayette* Flying Corps, Cpl David Endicott Putnam was briefly assigned to SPA94, then to MS156, where he was one of the few pilots to enjoy success in the Morane-Saulnier AI parasol monoplane. He then served with SPA38, learning tactics from Lt George Félix Madon, and raising his score to nine by the time he transferred to the 139th Aero Squadron in mid-June 1918. Putnam gained a further four confirmed victories with that unit, before being shot down and killed over Limey by Ltn Georg von Hantelmann of *Jasta* 15 on 12 September 1918

SPAD VII S2124 was assigned to Cpl Paul Frank Baer, a *Lafayette* Flying Corps volunteer attached to SPA80 who proclaimed his nationality by painting a draped American flag over the rear of the fighter's fuselage. The unit marking was a light blue band descending diagonally aft from below the cockpit

German fighters south of Armen-tiéres. The Americans immediately dived to attack, only to be 'bounced' in turn by three more Albatros scouts of *Jasta* 18, which had been waiting for them to do just that. Giroux was shot down and killed by Ltn Hans Müller. Baer in turn claimed an Albatros in flames, but his controls were then severed by bullets fired by Gefreiter Deberitz, and his fighter fell 4000 metres to crash-land near Laventie. The rest of the flight escaped the trap only with great difficulty.

Miraculously emerging from the crash with a broken knee, Baer was chivalrously hosted by his adversaries of *Jasta* 18, although he suffered rougher treatment at the hands of the infantrymen who conveyed him to prison – especially after he made an unsuccessful escape attempt.

Released on 19 January 1919, Baer duly received credit for his ninth victory. Continuing to pursue a career in aviation, he moved to China in 1930 to fly Loening amphibians, but was killed in an accident taking off from Shanghai on 9 December 1930.

Charles John Biddle was another American who had seen previous French service before joining the 103rd Aero Squadron, and although he scored less victories than Baer, he acquired more experience that would benefit not only him, but the USAS personnel he would later command. Born in Andalusia, Pennsylvania in 1890, and a graduate of Princeton University and the Harvard University of Law, Biddle had joined the LFC on 24 March 1917, and after training at Avord, he was assigned to SPA73 on 28 July.

After learning tactics under the tutelage of his commander, Lt Albert Deullin, Biddle was commissioned a captain in the USAS on 7 November, but remained with SPA73 until 10 January 1918, when he was assigned to SPA124. He was flying a new SPAD XIII when he scored his first victory over an Albatros two-seater near Langemarck on 5 December 1917, killing Ltns Fritz Pauly and Fritz Sauer of *Fl. Abt.* 45.

By the time Biddle arrived at SPA124, the unit was in the process of changing into an American squadron, which became official on 18 February 1918. In what might have seemed a retrograde step, he was assigned a SPAD VII, to which he stated that he applied 'a big blue band around the fuselage – and also a blue nose', as well as the Sioux insignia. He was flying this fighter when he scored his second victory over a Halberstadt CL II near Corbeny on 12 April 1918, killing Uffz Helmut Suhrmann and Ltn Theodor Krubek of *Fl. Abt.(A)* 201.

The 103rd moved to Leffrinckoucke, near Dunkirk, at the end of April, and Biddle had numerous other, less decisive encounters before running into an armoured Junkers J I reconnoitring over the lines between Langemarck and Ypres. He attacked, and was fortunate enough to describe what followed;

'He certainly got the best of me, and I don't feel at all vindictive about it, as it was a perfectly fair fight, but just the same it would give me more

A panel cut from the fuselage of SPAD VII S5301, which shows the evolution of the markings worn by fighters of the 103rd Aero Squadron between March and August 1918. The fighter from which this panel was taken was originally flown by Maj Thaw, and the fabric features the *Lafayette* Sioux head insignia, a variation on Bill Thaw's 'T' monogram in the form of a red and black medallion, overpainted with olive brown camouflage, and a chrome yellow number 11 adopted after the 103rd was transferred to the 2nd Pursuit Group, USAS. In addition to Thaw, S5301 was also flown by 1Lts Hobart A H Baker and Drummond Cannon (*Alan D Toelle via Jon Guttman*)

Slouch-hatted Australian troops examine SPAD S3173 of the 103rd Aero Squadron, which Paul Baer (by then a first lieutenant) used to down nine German aeroplanes to become the highest-scoring American SPAD VII ace

satisfaction to bring that boy down than any others. The observer did the quickest and most accurate shooting I have yet run up against, and his very first shot came crashing through the front of my machine above the motor and caught me just on the top of the left knee.'

His motor stopped, Biddle crash-landed less than 70 yards from the German lines, yet in spite of his knee wound, he succeeded in crawling, wading and sprinting several hundred yards to a British observation post. The observer who brought him down had indeed been a worthy opponent – Ltn Wilhelm Schreiber of *Fl. Abt.(A)* 221, who was credited with a SPAD while operating with his regular pilot, Feldwebel Ernst Schäfer, in Junkers J I 134/17. Soon after the engagement, Schreiber was recommended for the *Ordre Pour le Mérite* and Schäfer for the Golden *Militär-Verdeinstkreuz*, but both men were shot down and killed by ground fire on 30 May.

After recovering from his wound, Biddle returned to the front as commander of the newly-arrived 13th Aero Squadron, USAS, and flew SPAD XIIIs with that unit to raise his total to seven. On 25 October he was given command of the newly-formed 4th Pursuit Group, and finished the war as a major.

THE MERCURIOS

The only USAS aero squadron other than the 103rd to use SPAD VIIs in combat was the 139th, which was formed at Kelly Field, Texas, on 21 September 1917. Commanded by Maj Lawrence C Angstrom, the 139th Aero Squadron arrived in Britain on 5 March 1918, and after further training moved to Tours and then Vaucouleurs in France. Angstrom's flight leaders were all former volunteers with the French – Capts Ray Claflin Bridgman and Dudley L Hill were both veterans of the famed *Lafayette Escadrille*, while Capt David Putnam had scored nine victories with *escadrille*s MSP156 and SPA38.

On 29 June 1918, the 139th was joined by the 103rd Aero Squadron, which had detached from GC21 and been transferred to Vaucouleurs. Together with the 13th, 22nd and 49th Aero Squadrons, they formed the new 2nd Pursuit Group. The latter three units were equipping and training on the SPAD XIII, with 220-hp geared Hispano-Suiza 8Be engines and twin Vickers machine guns, but in the first month of the new group's existence it would be the SPAD VII-equipped 139th that would draw first blood.

One of the 139th's newer members was 1Lt Arthur Raymond Brooks. Born in Framingham, Massachusetts on 1 November 1895, Brooks had graduated from the Massachusetts Institute of Technology in 1917, and enlisted in the USAS that September. After training with the RFC in Toronto, Canada, and at Hicks Field, Texas,

Capt Charles J Biddle briefly experiments with a moustache while posing beside his SPAD VII of the 103rd Aero Squadron in the spring of 1918. Biddle described his aeroplane as having a blue band and cowling, although the photograph also shows an asymmetric white triangle on the fuselage upper decking, which some French pilots applied to throw off the aim of an enemy fighter on their tail (*The Lafayette Foundation*)

he was commissioned in February 1918, shipped out for France in March and completed his training at Issoudun. Brooks later described his first sorties with 'C' flight in the 139th Aero Squadron;

'Once assigned to a flight, I found myself under Putnam, and from the time we began operations my admiration grew, and my earliest successes were due entirely to such tactics as I learned with the leader.

'The first time he showed us the lines he took Lt Henry G MacLure and I for a trip over St Mihiel. Neither MacLure nor I had the faintest idea of what was going on. The first one or two trips were painful in their bewilderment. The flying is more or less mechanical, and one feels the need of a thousand eyes to take in the whole show. The war looked tame, yet there were the trenches and here we were above them, and the approach of a stranger flurried us not a little.

'Putnam, MacLure and I were on a voluntary patrol the first day after arriving at the Toul Airdrome. This was on 30 June, and during this ride I had a shot at my first Boche. A Rumpler biplane came sauntering over Viéville-en-Haye at 4500 meters. Putnam neatly reversed and lit into the two-seater, while I had a sparse three shots at the observer, who had his guns busy in the direction of Putnam. Putnam's bullets were effective and the Hun fell grotesquely, with portions of his aeroplane fluttering downward through the air. I fired some very close shots at the observer, and flew through the debris of the disintegrating aeroplane.

'Upon returning to the airdrome the Commander of the 8th French Army had sent congratulations along with the confirmation. Surely enough, that night there was a party in the Barracks.'

1Lt Arthur Raymond Brooks began his fighting career with the 139th Aero Squadron under the tutelage of his flight leader, 1Lt David Putnam. He opened his account with a Pfalz D III over Hendicourt on 29 July, and later downed a further five aircraft whilst flying SPAD XIIIs with the 22nd Aero Squadron

The 139th's first victory was Putnam's tenth overall, his victims being Sgt Eduard Bohlen and Ltn Gebhard Schia of *Fl. Abt.* 31.

'The squadron CO, Maj Angstrom, considered the Sector highly propitious for training a new unit to the actuality of Pursuit work', Brooks continued. 'It is true that before the St Mihiel drive, the Germans flew leisurely, and so did we. But, nevertheless, Putnam always managed two out of three times that we were on patrol to fall in with some excitement'.

Brooks recalled three Pfalz D IIIa fighters that repeatedly tried to bait Putnam's flight into venturing farther into enemy territory into what Brooks by then figured to be a trap. On at least one occasion, while protecting French artillery spotting aeroplanes, Putnam's flight engaged the trio. Brooks suffered a gun jam, and wound up with two enemy fighters on his tail. He managed shake them off, and saw Putnam diving with the third in pursuit. The latter escaped with his SPAD badly riddled, one bullet missing his leg by inches and others puncturing his main fuel tank.

'We were rather peevish with this episode, and it was therefore with great satisfaction that a few days later we met two of the same crew (we could tell from their markings), and I succeeded in "getting" one of them', Brooks continued. 'Putnam was leading Lt Adam H Fitzke and myself along the line from Fliry toward St Mihiel. I was on the leader's right. Suddenly, as always, the machine in front made its wings tremble and started in a beeline for two tiny specks in the distant haze. As we approached, I recognised two Hun *chasse* machines of previous acquaintance, so on the way we searched the heavens for that high third man. This fellow showed up later, after we were on our way home – he therefore played possum too far away.

'As we neared the enemy aircraft they dived sharply in a left turn. Putnam remained on his course. He was over the second of the two and I was over the first when he made a steep left dive and I did likewise. My Hun dived and I opened fire at 300 metres, and kept my tracers and bullets plowing the wings as I came down on this adversary. My engine choked and I momentarily levelled off. The Hun required no further attention, however, for he went down out of control.

'My engine picked up. I turned to see where Putnam was when "tack-tack-tack" – over my left lower wing was a little black beast spitting columns of white smoke at me. My thoughts at that first instant were that the fellow had knocked down my leader and then come for me. He did not allow enough deflection in his shooting, and quite unreservedly I called him names I wish he could have heard.

'Before I could get in position on his tail he swooped down through the lower layer of clouds and disappeared. I searched the air for Putnam, and with foreboding, headed home. There I found that he had had a gun jam and was obliged to withdraw and watch me. He offered comments on the scrap and was evidently delighted, and the episode was closed with the exception, however, that Fitzke had remained above the fight all this time, and in his newness never even saw the Huns, and for two days after presented himself gravely and asked to be kicked by each of the boys.

'As it happened, the Boche fell so far behind the lines that I could get no confirmation, and it was a strange way I received the credit for having shot down the enemy – through an observer on a reconnaissance tour spotting the crash a few days later.'

Ray Brooks was credited with a Pfalz at Heudicourt on 29 July, but its pilot apparently survived his crash-landing, since German records identify nobody killed or wounded in that area on the day. In any case, Brooks had gained a wealth of experience under Putnam, and on 16 August he was given command of 'C' Flight within the 22nd Aero Squadron, with whom he scored five more kills flying SPAD XIIIs. Putnam, too, would bring his total to 13 in SPAD XIIIs, but he was ultimately shot down and killed by Ltn Georg von Hantelmann of *Jasta* 15 on 12 September 1918.

Other future aces of the 139th, such as 1Lts John Sidney Owens and Karl Schoen Jr, gained their first frontline experience in SPAD VIIs, but unlike Putnam and Brooks, none of them scored any kills in the older fighters before their units, and the 103rd, began phasing them out as more SPAD XIIIs became available. Thanks to the successes of Putnam and Brooks, the 139th was also authorised to adopt a squadron insignia, which took the form of the wing-footed Roman messenger god Mercury, and the unit's pilots came to refer to themselves as the 'Mercurios'.

SPAD XIIIs had become the primary mounts of pilots of the 103rd by the time that unit resumed combat operations on 11 July, although 1Lt Van Winkle Todd was still flying one of the remaining SPAD VIIs (S3435) as late as 11 August, when he was brought down by an Albatros two-seater that he tried to engage and taken prisoner.

By that time, the 103rd had fallen fully under the auspices of the USAS, which compelled the unit to conform to a uniform system of markings that saw the old personal emblems of the unit's *Lafayette* days replaced by yellow numbers. In an interesting emulation of GC12 and GC21 policy, however, Maj Thaw arranged for the 103rd to become the nucleus of his new group after he was made CO of the 103rd Pursuit Group on 30 July. And he subsequently adopted different styles of Indian heads as insignias for the others three units (the 28th, 93rd and 213th Aero Squadrons).

SPAD VIIs made a final appearance in the USAS as equipment for the 41st, 138th and 638th Aero Squadrons of the 5th Fighter Group in October 1918, but the war ended before the newly-organised unit commenced operations.

The SPAD XIII remains the fighter most widely associated with the USAS. Nevertheless, a lot of its leading American exponents could claim to have first cut their teeth on its precursor – and added their country to a remarkable variety of others whose pilots flew the SPAD VII to fame in World War 1.

Brooks sits in his de Marçay-built SPAD VII, S7144, which he named *Smith I* after Smith College, where his girlfriend had been a student. American cockades appear on the upper wing, but the rudder still had French stripes. Also of note are the absence of cowling panels, the rear-view mirror immediately above the pilot's head, and the teddy bear mascot perched on the upper wing. The 139th Aero Squadron's Mercury insignia was not applied to its aircraft until after the unit had received SPAD XIIIs in August 1918

APPENDICES

French Air Force SPAD VII *Escadrille* in 1916-18

SPA3, SPA12, SPA15, SPA23, SPA26, SPA31, SPA37, SPA38, SPA48, SPA49, SPA57, SPA62, SPA65, SPA67, SPA68, SPA69, SPA73, SPA75, SPA76, SPA77, SPA78, SPA79, SPA80, SPA81, SPA82, SPA83, SPA84, SPA85, SPA86, N87, SPA88, SPA89, N92, SPA94, SPA95, SPA96, SPA97, SPA98, SPA99, SPA100, SPA102, SPA103, SPA112, SPA124, SPA150, SPA151, SPA152, SPA153, SPA154, SPA155, SPA156, SPA157, SPA158, SPA159, SPA160, SPA161, SPA162, SPA163, SPA315, N392, SPA531, SPA561, N581

RFC SPAD VII Squadrons in France in 1917-18

No 19 Sqn, February 1917 – January 1918
No 23 Sqn, February 1917 – December 1917

United States Air Service SPAD VII Aero Squadrons in France in 1918

41st, 103rd, 138th, 139th, 141st, 638th

Belgian Air Force SPAD VII *Escadrille* in 1917-18

5ème (later *10ème*) *Escadrille*, July 1917 – November 1918

Italian SPAD VII *Squadriglie* in 1917-18

77ª, March 1917 – November 1918
91ª, May 1917 – November 1918

(in addition, *70ª*, *71ª*, *75ª*, *76ª*, *78ª*, *82ª*, *83ª* and *84ª* *Squadriglie* were partially equipped with SPAD VIIs at some time during the war)

Russian Air Service SPAD VII Squadrons in 1917

7, XI, XIX Fighter Detachments

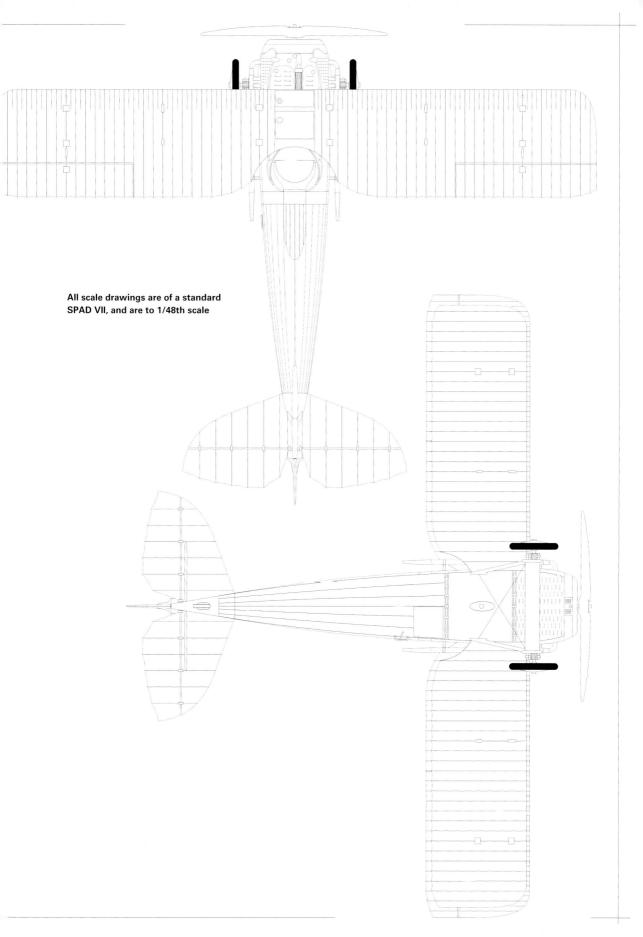

All scale drawings are of a standard
SPAD VII, and are to 1/48th scale

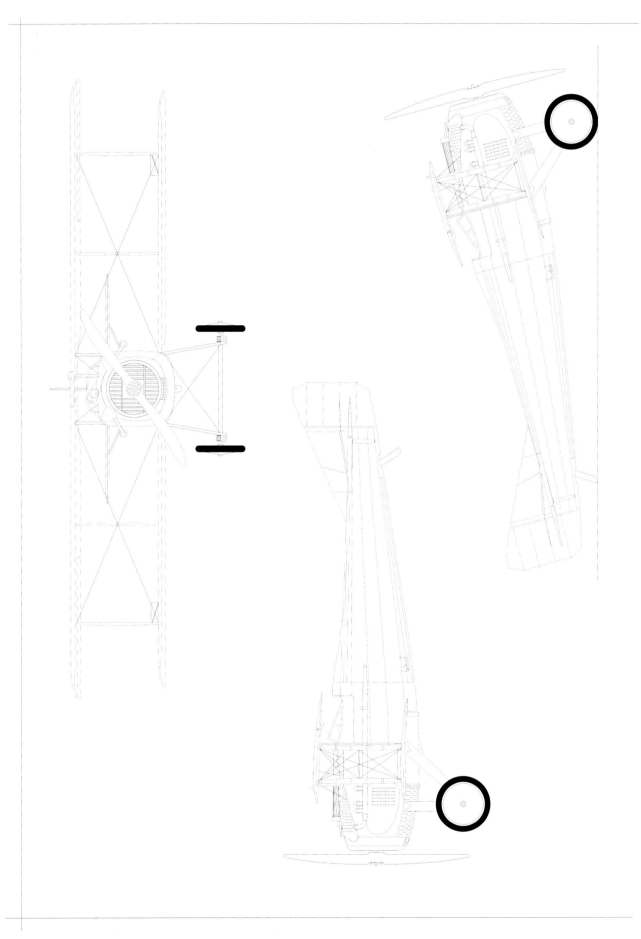

1

SPAD VII S115 of Sgt Georges Guynemer, N3, September 1916

Guynemer's first SPAD VII arrived on 27 August 1916, and it was decorated with a black pennant on the fuselage upper decking and *"Vieux Charles"* on the fuselage side. If the tricolour fuselage band was meant to identify the new aeroplane to French soldiers, it did not work very well, for S115 was written off after being brought down on 23 September – by a French 75 mm shell. Also see Upper View 1.

2

SPAD VII (serial unknown) of Lt Alfred Heurtaux, N3, Autumn 1916

Only a red stork and numeral adorned the fuselage of Heurtaux's SPAD. Amongst the 21 opponents that the Frenchman 'bested' in combat during the course of his career was German ace Ltn Kurt Wintgens, who was shot down and killed on 25 September 1916.

3

SPAD VII S314 of Sous-Lt René Dorme, SPA3, Spring 1917

In addition to his usual number 12 – albeit in a relatively small size – and his nickname on the fuselage side, Dorme's SPAD VII had a green cross of Lorraine on the upper decking. Dorme scored 23 official victories – and numerous others that went unconfirmed – before being killed in action on 25 May 1917, his demise giving Ltn Heinrich Kroll of *Jasta* 9 his all-important fifth victory.

4

SPAD VII S116 of Adjutant Maxime Lenoir, N23, October 1916

Personal heraldry predominated on the aircraft of N23 throughout the war, Lenoir's including a tricolour band, a rebus on his own name and a death-defying legend that proved to be premature. After scoring his 11th victory on 25 September 1916, Lenoir was killed in his new SPAD exactly one month later.

5

SPAD VII (serial unknown) of Sous-Lt Georges Ortoli, SPA31, Spring 1917

Corsican ace Georges Ortoli scored his first victory while flying a Maurice Farman pusher with MF8, followed by ten more in Nieuports and SPAD VIIs with SPA31. His best month was March 1917, in which he downed single enemy aircraft on the 6th, 23rd and 24th, and two on 25th. He claimed another double on 19 June, one of which was shared with Sous-Lt Jean Chaput of SPA57 and Lt Xavier de Sevin of SPA12.

6

SPAD VII S1165 of Adjutant Hector Garaud, SPA38, Summer 1917

Hector Garaud's SPAD carried a variation on the black thistle emblem and motto ('Whoever rubs up against me gets pricked') of SPA38's leading ace, Georges Madon – this marking was adopted by the entire *escadrille*. That, and personal variations on red and white bands, were later combined into a triangular pennant in 1918, with conventional numerals used for individual identification. Garaud scored a total of six victories during the course of 1917, and increased his final tally to 13 on 12 August 1918.

7

SPAD VII S1213 of Cpl Jacques Roques, SPA48, Summer 1917

Born in Paris on 2 August 1897, Roques was a Swiss citizen who joined the *Aviation Français* via the Foreign Legion. In addition to the standard SPA48 cockerel's head and number 7, he decorated his second SPAD VII with a *'jolie demoiselle'* devised by his friend, Parisian artist Georges Lepape. Roques scored two of his five victories in SPAD VIIs – an Albatros shared with Sgt Robert Bajac on 26 April 1917, and an unidentifed German fighter shared with Bajac and Sous-Lt Georges Ortoli of SPA31 on 27 July.

8

SPAD VII S4280 of Lt Jean Chaput, SPA57, May 1918

Chaput's 16 victories included 10-kill German ace Ltn Erich Thomas of *Jasta* 22, who was brought down and taken prisoner on 23 March 1918. Taking command of SPA57 on 11 April 1918, his personal seagull marking was soon adopted as the unit insignia in place of the unpopular wild boar motif that had been in use since 1917. Chaput was flying S4280 on 6 May 1918 when he was mortally wounded in the femoral artery during a fight with a Fokker Dr I flown by Ltn Hermann Becker, CO of *Jasta* 12.

9

SPAD VII (serial unknown) of Sous-Lt Marius Hasdenteufel, SPA57, June 1918

Hasdenteufel was probably flying this Marçay-built machine when he scored his fifth victory in concert with Sous-Lt Charles Nuville on 25 June 1918. The newly-crowned ace was killed in a flying accident the very next day.

10

SPAD VII S5325 of Sgt André Bosson, SPA62, May 1918

Born in Esmans (Seine-et-Marne) on 1 June 1894 to Swiss parents, André Louis Bosson enlisted in the French army on 6 September 1914, and transferred to the air service in 1917 – he was the only non-French citizen to enter the military without first joining the Foreign Legion. Sent to SPA62 on Christmas Eve 1917, Bosson scored seven victories between 9 March and 4 June 1918, but on 20 July he was mortally wounded by German ground fire whilst at the controls of de Marçay-built SPAD VII S5325 east of Hartennes.

11

SPAD VII S4236 of Sgt Jacques Gerard, SPA65, Winter 1918

Probably used by Sgt Jacques Gerard to score his first victory, in concert with Sous-Lt André Borde, on 30 January 1918, this SPAD displays the later dark blue dragon and Arabic numerals adopted by SPA65 in late 1917. Gerard would go on to score eight victories before being killed in action on 3 July 1918.

12

SPAD VII S2124 of Cpl Paul Frank Baer, SPA80, Winter 1917

A *Lafayette* Flying Corps volunteer attached to SPA80, Baer graphically proclaimed his nationality by painting a draped American flag over the rear of fuselage. The unit marking was a blue band descending diagonally aft from below the cockpit.

13 and 13A

SPAD VII (serial unknown) of Lt Jacques Leps, SPA81, April 1917

A St-Cyr graduate, Jacques Leps was transferred from the *9e* to the *1e Régiment de Hussards* on 4 November 1914. Honouring the latter regiment, the ace had the unit's pre-Napoleonic name applied to each side of his fighter's fuselage. Aside from these personal markings, the SPAD VII also featured the more standard red-white-red wing stripes that identified machines assigned to SPA81 in early 1917. Having joined SPA81 on 14 December 1916, Leps was eventually placed in command of the squadron on 24 February 1918, and he finished the war with 12 victories. He subsequently served as a commandant within GC21 during World War 2, and retired as a Lieutenant-colonel and *Commandeur de la Légion d'Honneur*. Also see Upper View 2.

14

SPAD VII (serial unknown) of Adjutant Edmond Pillon, SPA82, September 1917

Like N81, N82 initially identified itself with red and white wing bands, later switching to a red and white banded pennant with a cockerel's head. A former bomber pilot with VB102 (with whom he had scored his first victory on 2 August 1916), Edmond Jacques Marcel Pillon transferred to the newly-formed N82 on 1 January 1917. Flying Nieuports, he downed three aeroplanes between 25 March and 24 April 1917, and added at least one to his score during a welter of activity in August and September 1917 while using the 180-hp SPAD VII. Pillon was wounded on 10 September, although he returned to combat with SPA67 on 15 April 1918 and scored two more kills, plus one with SPA98. Also see Upper View 3.

15

SPAD VII (serial unknown) of Sous-Lt Omer Demeuldre, SPA84, Spring 1918

Demeuldre scored his first victory whilst serving as the gunner of a Maurice Farman from MF63 on 7 September 1915, and his second as a pilot with the same unit on 23 May 1917. Training as a fighter pilot that October, the aggressive Demeuldre joined SPA84 and scored his third victory in a SPAD VII on the 30th of that month. A German two-seater downed on 14 April 1918 brought his tally up to 13, but on 3 May he was killed in combat with another two-seater, after which he was posthumously made a *Chevalier de la Légion d'Honneur*. Also see Upper View 4.

16

SPAD VII (serial unknown) of Adjutant André Martenot de Cordoux, SPA94, Spring 1918

Martenot, who scored his first victory flying a Caudron G IV with C28, was the most experienced member of N94 when that unit was formed on 1 June 1917, and consequently received its first SPAD VII (S135) in July. His aircraft all bore the numeral '5', and he stated that his favourite SPAD VII – the pennant of which he kept and later donated to the *Musée de l'Air* – had a polished aluminium radiator cowling. He preferred the SPAD VII to the more powerful but less reliable and manoeuvrable XIII, and flew both for a time, eventually being credited with eight victories.

17

SPAD VII S1461 of Sous-Lt René Fonck, SPA103, Summer 1917

Fonck's S1461 is notable for the extra perforations cut into the forward fuselage ahead of the cowling louvres, these being added in an effort to help cool the fighter's notoriously hot-running engine. Just visible on the upper wing is the old red star of N103, and the fuselage side shows Fonck's red number IX superimposed on an overpainted number XV. Also see Upper View 5.

18

SPAD VII (serial unknown) of Sgt Victor Régnier, SPA112, Spring 1917

A typical SPA112 machine, this SPAD has the unit's distinctive twin red fuselage bands. Its pilot, Victor Régnier, had served in the *2e Régiment d'Artillerie de Montagne* up until he was wounded on 29 March 1915. Transferring to aviation on 1 September, one of his SPAD VIIs consequently bore two crossed black cannon silhouettes on its fuselage sides, forward of the red bands. His first kill was scored in concert with Adjutant Norman Prince of N124 on 9 September 1916, and soon after becoming an ace (following the destruction of a balloon) on 6 April 1917, Régnier was severely wounded and evacuated to the rear.

19

SPAD VII S1456 of Lt William Thaw, SPA124, June 1917

Several members of the *Lafayette Escadrille* identified themselves with initials or monograms on both Nieuports and SPADs. Thaw was flying a Nieuport 11 when he downed a Fokker E III on 24 May 1916, and then used a SPAD VII to score his second victory (an Albatros two-seater) over Neuville on 26 April 1917.

20

SPAD VII S1777 of Sous-Lt G Raoul Lufbery, SPA124, December 1917

Although this particular SPAD (S1777) was most associated with Didier Masson, who flew 20 missions with it, the veteran fighter was also flown by ten other pilots, including Sous-Lt Lufbery. He completed 26 missions in the scout, including one on 24 October 1917 in which he and Lt Paul Louis Malavialle of SPA69 downed a German two-seater over Courtecon for Lufbery's 14th and Malavialle's fifth, and final, victory. Lufbery was flying S1777 again on 2 December, when he teamed up with four pilots from SPA88 to down another two-seater south of Ployart, and then dispatched a second over Laval for his 16th, and final, victory. Also see Upper View 6.

21
SPAD VII S1783 of Maréchal-des-Logis Louis Moissinac, SPA154, Spring 1918

SPA154's markings consisted of a red fuselage band and a red radiator cowling, with individual markings generally limited to serial numbers – although a few pilots added names under the cockpit. Starting with a 'double' over a balloon and an enemy aeroplane on 1 April 1918, Xavier Jean-Marie Louis Moissinac scored seven victories before being killed in action on 3 June 1918.

22
SPAD VII (serial unknown) of 1Lt Thomas G Cassady, SPA163, Spring 1918

Although *Lafayette* Flying Corps member Thomas G Cassady was transferred to the USAS and commissioned a first lieutenant in February 1918, he was assigned to SPA163 from 14 May to 8 September 1918. During that time he downed five enemy aeroplanes, then brought his combat experience to the 28th Aero Squadron as a flight leader – where he added a further four victories to his score. Cassady later worked for the French Resistance and the Office of Strategic Services during World War 2.

23
SPAD VII (serial unknown) of Sous-Lt Georges Lachmann, N581, Autumn 1917

Lachmann flew this SPAD from Kamnietz-Padolsk airfield in Russia. In addition to its synchronised Vickers machine gun, he added a Lewis gun on a makeshift overwing mounting and occasionally Le Prieur rockets for balloon-busting missions. Three of his five successes in Russia were against balloons.

24
SPAD VII (serial unknown) of Sous-Lt Louis Coudouret, N581, Autumn 1917

Like Lachmann, Sous-Lt Louis Fernand Coudouret served in *Escadrille* N57 as well as N102, scoring a victory in each unit, before being assigned to the French Aeronautic Mission to Russia. He claimed three kills in Russia with N581 and then returned to France, where he scored his sixth, and final, victory with SPA103.

25
SPAD VII A.6663 of Lt Augustus H Orlebar, No 19 Sqn, March 1917

SPAD VII A.6663 displays the dumb-bell marking that appeared at various times on aircraft of No 19 Sqn in March 1917. A veteran of the Gallipoli debacle (where he was wounded by a Turkish sniper), Augustus Henry Orlebar was flying A.6663 when he claimed a Halberstadt scout that could not be confirmed on 24 March 1917, destroyed an Albatros D III in flames east of Douai on 23 May and sent another down out of control on 5 June. Later, while flying Sopwith Camels with No 73 Sqn, Orlebar claimed an Albatros D V and a Fokker Dr I on 13 March 1918 – the latter was being flown by Ltn Lothar von Richthofen of *Jasta* 11, who crash-landed and was severely wounded. Orlebar downed two more Albatros D Vs on 22 March, and brought his total to seven with a Fokker D VII while flying a Sopwith Snipe in No 43 Sqn on 29 September 1918.

26
SPAD VII B.1537 of Lt James M Child, No 19 Sqn, May 1917

In late April 1917, the black dumb-bell was replaced on No 19 Sqn SPADs by blue, white and red bands and wheel discs in an attempt to facilitate better identification in the air. Child used B.1537 to destroy an Albatros two-seater north-west of Douai on 27 April and to send an Albatros D III down out of control west of Douai on 25 May. His final tally of eight included three kills in SPADs and five in SE 5as with No 84 Sqn.

27
SPAD VII A.6662 of 2Lt Richard A Hewat, No 19 Sqn, October 1917

A British-built SPAD, A.6662 features PC.10 camouflaged uppersurfaces. Canadian Richard Alexander Hewat was flying this machine on 30 September 1917 when he and four other pilots sent a two-seater down out of control over Gheluwe. He then shared in driving an Albatros two-seater down out of control on 9 October, and downed another two-seater on 26 October, but was wounded in the head by machine gun fire from the ground while returning from that mission at an altitude of just 200 ft. Upon recovery, Hewat returned to combat in Sopwith Dolphins with No 87 Sqn, with whom he added three more victories to his tally. However, on 14 August 1918 he was killed in Dolphin D4434, having probably fallen victim to Lt d R Hermann Leptien of *Jasta* 63.

28
SPAD VII B.1524 of Capt William J C K Cochran-Patrick, No 23 Sqn, April 1917

Future 21-kill ace Capt William J C K Cochran-Patrick was flying B.1524 when he drove two Albatros D IIIs down out of control on 22 April 1917, followed by a two-seater four days later. However, the tables were turned on B.1524 on 7 June when a wounded 2Lt F W Illingworth force-landed it near Menin and was taken prisoner. His opponent had been Offizierstellvertreter Paul Aue of *Jasta* 10.

29
SPAD VII A.253 of Capt Ernest L Foot, No 60 Sqn, September 1916

Delivered to No 2 Aircraft Depot, Candas, on 9 September 1916, SPAD VII S126 was given the RFC serial A.253 and assigned to No 60 Sqn for evaluation on 20 September. Eight days later it became the first British SPAD to achieve success when Capt Ernest L Foot destroyed an Albatros two-seater over Avesnes les Bapaume for his fourth victory.

30
SPAD VII (serial unknown) of Sous-Lt Edmond Thieffry, *5ème Escadrille Belge*, Autumn 1917

In mid-August 1917, Thieffry received the first Belgian SPAD VII (Sp 1), which was probably decorated with the unit's comet emblem and Thieffry's red and white bands prior to it being written-off in combat on 31 August. His second fighter received even more flamboyant treatment, and was used by him to score his tenth, and final, confirmed victory on 16 October, as well as a 'probable' on 6 November. Thieffry was subsequently shot down and taken prisoner on 23 February 1918.

31
SPAD VII (serial unknown) of Stabs-Rotmistre Aleksandr A Kozakov, 1st Combat Air Group, Autumn 1917

In contrast to the remaining aircraft within his famous 19th Detachment, which had white skulls on black rudders, Kozakov's SPAD bore a black skull and crossbones on a white rudder. The fighter's cowl stripes have been variously described as dark blue and gold – in reference to Kozakov's former cavalry unit – or red and blue. In any case, the Russian ace scored none of his 20 kills in the SPAD, often letting his deputy, Esaul (Cossack captain) Shangin fly it instead while he stuck to his Nieuport 17. Shangin was finally brought down in this aeroplane by Austro-Hungarian fighters on 12 September 1917, the Russian becoming a PoW. Also see Upper View 7.

32
SPAD VII (serial unknown) of Praporshik Ivan V Smirnov, 19th Detachment, Autumn 1917

Smirnov scored seven of his eleven confirmed victories flying the SPAD VII in 1917, despite the old Imperial Russian order that he faithfully served falling to revolution.

33
SPAD VII (serial unknown) of Tenente Carlo Francesco Lombardi, *77ª Squadriglia*, Spring 1918

Most SPAD VIIs of *77ª Squadriglia* wore a large red heart in a white disk aft of the cockpit, but *'Il Piccinin'* ('Kid') Lombardi flew at least one with a fuselage cockade preceding the squadron insignia. Besides being an eight-victory ace, Lombardi achieved fame for three long-distance flights and for forming the Avia company in 1938.

34
SPAD VII S1420 of Sergente Maggiore Ernesto Cabruna, *77ª Squadriglia*, Autumn 1918

Cabruna decorated his SPAD VII with the crest of Tortona. Following the armistice, his aeroplane was also marked with the Roman numeral 'XIII' on both upper wings and nine black crosses on the fuselage decking, although only eight of these kills were confirmed. S1420 is currently displayed at the Italian Air Force Museum at Vigna di Valle, near Rome.

35
SPAD VII (serial unknown) of Tenente Ferruccio Ranza, *91ª Squadriglia*, Summer 1917

Yet another paladin of Baracca's *91ª Squadriglia* was Tenente Ferruccio Ranza, who scored four victories in Nieuport 11s with *77ª Squadriglia* before transferring to *91ª* in early June 1917, and bringing his total to 17 by 17 August 1918.

36
SPAD VII (serial unknown) of Capitano Fulco Ruffo di Calabria, *91ª Squadriglia*, Summer 1917

After scoring eight kills in Nieuports with *70ª* and *91ª Squadriglie*, Capitano di Calabria downed another 12 aircraft in SPADs. All of his scouts were marked with a black death's head, this version being applied over the fuselage cockade.

37
SPAD VII (serial unknown) of Capitano Fulco Ruffo di Calabria, *91ª Squadriglia*, October 1917

A later, more sinister looking, variation of Calabria's death's head motif graced this SPAD VII come the autumn of 1917.

38 and 38A
SPAD VII (serial unknown) of Capitano Francesco Baracca, *91ª Squadriglia*, October 1917

One of Baracca's SPADs is known to have had his *cavallino rampante* personal emblem on one side of the fuselage and the newly-adopted griffon squadron insignia on the other.

39
SPAD VII (serial unknown) of Capt Charles J Biddle, 103rd Aero Squadron, April 1918

Charles Biddle scored his first victory with a SPAD XIII in French *Escadrille* SPA73, but was flying a SPAD VII with the 103rd Aero Squadron when he gained his second over a Halberstadt CL II near Corbeny on 12 April 1918. The scheme worn by Biddle's SPAD VII (which has been reconstructed from a partial photograph, as well as from his own description) included an asymmetrical, triangular, white pennant on the upper fuselage decking that some French pilots applied in the hope of putting an enemy pilot on their tails off his aim. Biddle brought his final total to seven flying SPAD XIIIs as CO of the 13th Aero Squadron. Also see also upper view 8.

40
SPAD VII S3173 of 1Lt Paul F Baer, 103rd Aero Squadron, May 1918

Another former *Lafayette* Flying Corps volunteer, Baer became the highest-scoring SPAD VII pilot in the USAS by downing nine German aeroplanes between 11 March and 22 May 1918. However, on the latter date he was shot down in S3173 by Gefreiter Deberitz of *Jasta* 18 and taken prisoner.

41
SPAD VII S5301 of Capt William Thaw, 103rd Aero Squadron, Spring 1918

Originally assigned to Bill Thaw on 27 February 1918, this fighter was decorated not only with the *Lafayette* Sioux head insignia, but also a variation on Thaw's 'T' monogram in the form of a red and black medallion. S5301 was subsequently assigned to another pilot in May, and a chrome yellow number '5' painted in front of Thaw's marking. Later still, the '5' was overpainted with brown and replaced with the number 11. In addition to Thaw, S5301 is known to have been flown by 1Lts Hobart A H Baker and Drummond Cannon before being turned in on 16 June 1918.

42
SPAD VII S7144 of 1Lt Arthur Raymond Brooks, 139th Aero Squadron, June 1918

Ray Brooks named his de Marçay-built SPAD VII *Smith I* after Smith College, where his girlfriend had been a pupil. American cockades appear on the upper wing, but the rudder still has French stripes. Personal touches included a red number 7 outlined in white and a teddy bear on the upper wing. The 139's Mercury insignia was not applied until the unit received SPAD XIIIs in August. Brooks opened his account with a Pfalz D III over Hendicourt on 29 July, and later downed a further five aircraft flying SPAD XIIIs with the 22nd Aero Squadron.

Bailey, Frank W, *The 103rd Aero, USAS (Formerly Lafayette Escadrille).* Cross & Cockade (USA) Journal, Vol 19, No 4, Winter 1978

Davila, James and Arthur M Soltan, *French Aircraft of the First World War.* Flying Machines Press, Stratford, Connecticut, 1997

Fonck, Capt René, *Ace of Aces.* Doubleday & Company, Inc, New York, New York, 1967

Franks, Norman, Russell Guest and Gregory Alegi, *Above the War Fronts.* Grub Street, London, 1997

Franks, Norman and Frank W Bailey, *Over the Front.* Grub Street, London, 1992

Guttman, Jon, *Interviews with Pierre de Cazenove de Pradines and Pierre Cardon.* Cross & Cockade Journal (USA), Vol 21, No 1, Spring 1980

Harnish, Herb, *The Paul Baer Scrapbook.* Fort Wayne Historical Society, 1968

Kilduff, Peter, *'That's My Bloody Plane'.* The Pequot Press, Chester, Conn, 1975

Kroll, Heinrich, *'A Fighter Pilot on the Western Front'.* Cross & Cockade (USA) Journal, Vol 14, No 2, p 181

La Vie Aérienne Illustrée, 1917-18

Lombardi, Francis, *'Gli Amici di Marcon – 1918-1978'.* Cross & Cockade (Great Britain) Journal, Vol 12, No 3, pp 118-129

Porret, Daniel, *Les 'As' français de la Grande Guerre.* Service Historique de l'Armée de l'Air, Château de Vincennes, 1983

Robertson, Bruce, *'Fighting Colours, 1914-1937, Part 6: French Fighters in British Service'.* Airfix Magazine, December 1972, pp 214-216

Schaedel, Charles, *Australian Air Ace: The Exploits of 'Jerry' Pentland, MC, DFC, AFC.* Rigby Ltd, Adelaide, 1979

Woolley, Charles, *'Pages du Gloire: A Brief History of Escadrille 3',* Cross & Cockade (USA) Journal, Vol 15 No 1, Spring 1974, pp 27-62

INDEX

References to illustrations are shown in **bold**. Plates are shown with page and caption locators in brackets, Upper View plates being pre-fixed 'UV'.